GCSE OCR 21st Century
Core Science
The Revision Guide

This book is for anyone doing **GCSE OCR 21st Century Core Science** at higher level.

GCSE Science is all about **understanding how science works**.
And not only that — understanding it well enough to be able to **question**
what you hear on TV and read in the papers.

But you can't do that without a fair chunk of **background knowledge**. Hmm, tricky.

Happily this CGP book includes all the **science facts** you need to learn,
and shows you how they work in the **real world**. And in true CGP style,
we've explained it all as **clearly and concisely** as possible.

It's also got some daft bits in to try and make the whole
experience at least vaguely entertaining for you.

What CGP is all about

Our sole aim here at CGP is to produce the highest
quality books — carefully written, immaculately presented
and dangerously close to being funny.

Then we work our socks off to get them out to you — at the cheapest possible prices.

Contents

HOW SCIENCE WORKS

The Scientific Process 1
Correlation and Cause 3
Risk 4
Science Has Limits 5

MODULE B1 — YOU AND YOUR GENES

Genes, Chromosomes and DNA 6
Genes and Variation 7
Inheritance 8
Girl or Boy? 9
Inheritance and Environment 10
Clones 11
Genetic Disorders 12
Genetic Testing 13
Gene Therapy and Ethics 14
Stem Cells 15
Science and Ethics 16
Revision Summary for Module B1 17

MODULE C1 — AIR QUALITY

Chemicals From The Earth 18
Chemical Reactions: Combustion 19
Fuels and Pollutants 20
Pollution: Carbon 21
Pollution: Sulfur 22
Pollution: Nitrogen 23
Interpreting Pollution Data 24
Reducing Pollution 25
Sustainable Development 26
Revision Summary for Module C1 27

MODULE P1 — THE EARTH IN THE UNIVERSE

The Changing Earth 28
Observations and Explanations 29
The Structure of the Earth 30
The Solar System 31
Danger from Space 32
Beyond the Solar System 33
Looking into Space 34
The Life Cycle of Stars 35
The Life of the Universe 36
The Scientific Community 37
Revision Summary for Module P1 38

MODULE B2 — KEEPING HEALTHY

Microorganisms and Disease 39
The Immune System 40
Vaccination 41
Vaccination Pros and Cons 42
Antibiotics 43
Drug Trials 44
The Circulatory System 45
Heart Disease 46
Correlation and Cause 47
Revision Summary for Module B2 48

MODULE C2 —
MATERIAL CHOICES

Natural and Synthetic Materials 49
Materials and Properties 50
Making Measurements 51
Materials, Properties and Uses 52
Chemical Synthesis 53
Polymerisation 54
Structures and Properties of Polymers 55
Life Cycle Assessments 56
Revision Summary for Module C2 57

MODULE P2 —
RADIATION AND LIFE

Electromagnetic Radiation 58
EM Radiation and Energy 59
Ionisation 60
Some Uses of EM Radiation 61
EM Radiation and Life 62
EM Radiation and The Atmosphere 63
The Carbon Cycle 64
Climate Change 65
Risks from EM Radiation 66
Revision Summary for Module P2 67

MODULE B3 —
LIFE ON EARTH

Evolution 68
Natural Selection 69
Producing New Species 70
A Scientific Controversy 71
Human Evolution 72
The Nervous System 73
Hormones 74
Interdependence 75
Humans and the Earth 76
Revision Summary for Module B3 77

MODULE C3 —
FOOD MATTERS

Recycling Elements 78
Organic and Intensive Farming 79
Natural Polymers 81
Digestion 82
Insulin and Diabetes 83
Harmful Chemicals in Food 84
Food Additives 85
Keeping Food Safe 86
Eating Healthily 87
Revision Summary for Module C3 88

MODULE P3 —
RADIOACTIVE MATERIALS

Radioactivity 89
The Three Kinds of Nuclear Radiation 90
Half-Life 91
Danger from Nuclear Radiation 92
Using Nuclear Radiation 93
Radiation and Risk 94
Electricity 95
Generating Electricity 96
Electricity from Nuclear Fuels 97
Electricity in the Future 98
Revision Summary for Module P3 99

Exam Skills 100
Answers 104
Index 105

Published by Coordination Group Publications Ltd.

Editors:
Sarah Hilton, Kate Houghton, Andy Park, Kate Redmond, Rachel Selway,
Jennifer Underwood, Julie Wakeling.

Contributors:
Mike Bossart, James Foster, Gemma Hallam, Derek Harvey, John Myers, Richard Parsons,
Andy Rankin, Adrian Schmit, Moira Steven, Emma Stevens, Paul Warren, Andy Williams.

ISBN-10: 1 84146 622 0
ISBN-13: 978 1 84146 622 4

With thanks to Philip Dobson, Ian Francis, Sue Hocking, and Glenn Rogers for the proofreading.
With thanks to Katie Steele for the copyright research.

Data used to construct table on page 92 from World Nuclear Association:
www.world-nuclear.org/info/inf05.htm

With thanks to Science Photo Library for permission to reproduce the images used on pages
18, 25, 28, 54, 60, 65 and 76

Groovy website: www.cgpbooks.co.uk

Printed by Elanders Hindson Ltd, Newcastle upon Tyne.
Jolly bits of clipart from CorelDRAW®

The Scientific Process

This section isn't about how to 'do' science — but it does show you the way most scientists work, and how scientists try to find decent explanations for things that happen. It's pretty important stuff.

Scientists Come Up with Hypotheses...

1) Scientists try to explain things. Everything.

2) Scientists start by observing or thinking about something they don't understand. It could be anything, e.g. planets in the sky, a person suffering from an illness, what matter is made of... anything.

About 100 years ago, we thought atoms looked like this.

3) Then, using what they already know (plus a lot of creativity and insight), they work out an explanation that could explain what they've observed. Then they think of a hypothesis (a prediction) that can be tested to see if there is any evidence to support the explanation. There are loads of people who can collect data perfectly well, but far fewer who can come up with a decent explanation that stands up to the next stage of the scientific process — scrutiny from other scientists.

...Then Those Hypotheses are Tested

1) A hypothesis is basically just a prediction about what might happen. And predicting what will happen doesn't mean it will happen — not even if you're a scientist.

2) So the next step is to try and find evidence to support the hypothesis.

3) There are lots of different types of evidence:

- Results from controlled experiments in laboratories are great — a lab makes it easy to control variables so they're all kept constant (except the one you're investigating) — so it's easier to carry out a fair test.

- Data can also come from studies, e.g. of populations or samples of a population, or from observations, e.g. of the movement of planets, or of animal behaviour.

- The evidence might already be out there — the scientist might analyse existing data from a previous experiment to test the hypothesis.

- Rumours, hearsay and evidence from very small samples should all be taken with a pinch of salt — they're not very reliable.

Other Scientists Will Test the Hypotheses Too

1) Scientists report their findings to other scientists, e.g. by publishing their results in journals. Other scientists will use the evidence to make their own predictions, and they'll carry out their own experiments. (They'll also try to reproduce earlier results.) And if all the experiments back up the hypothesis, then scientists start to have a lot of faith in it, and accept it as a theory.

Then we thought they looked like this.

2) However, if a scientist somewhere in the world does an experiment that doesn't fit with the hypothesis (and other scientists can reproduce these new results), then the explanation is in trouble. When this happens, scientists have to come up with a new hypothesis (maybe a modification of the old explanation, or maybe a completely new one).

3) This process of testing a hypothesis to destruction is a vital part of the scientific process. Without the 'healthy scepticism' of scientists everywhere, we'd still believe the first theories that people came up with — like thunder being the belchings of an angered god (or whatever).

Science is a "real-world" subject...

Science isn't just about explaining things that people are curious about — if scientists can explain something that happens in the world, then maybe they can predict what will happen in the future, or even control future events — to make life a bit better in some way, either for themselves or for other people.

The Scientific Process

Evidence is the key to science — but not all evidence is equally good.
The way evidence is gathered can have a big effect on how trustworthy it is...

Evidence Is Only Reliable If Other People Can Repeat It

Scientific evidence needs to be reliable (or reproducible). If it isn't, then it doesn't really help.

> RELIABLE means that the data can be reproduced by others.

> In 1989, two scientists claimed that they'd produced 'cold fusion' (the energy source of the Sun — but without the enormous temperatures). It was huge news — if true, this could have meant energy from seawater — the ideal energy solution for the world... forever. However, other scientists just couldn't get the same results — i.e. the results weren't reliable. And until they are, 'cold fusion' isn't going to be generally accepted as fact.

Measurements Aren't Always Accurate

You can't be sure that your measurements are accurate:

1) If you take a lot of measurements of the same thing, you won't always get the same result.

2) This might be because you're measuring lots of individual things, e.g. the height of plants.
   Or the thing that you're measuring might not always be the same, e.g. the pollution level in the air.

3) It might be because your measuring equipment isn't accurate, or you're not very good at measuring.

4) The best way to get an accurate result is to repeat the measurement lots of times. The values that you get should all fall into a range that shows roughly where the real value is. If you've got measurements that are obviously outside that range, then there's a chance that something has gone wrong with the measurement. Then you can take a mean (average) of your results — see page 51 for more on this.

You have to Watch Out for Bias

1) Scientific results are sometimes presented in a biased way — you need to be able to spot that.

2) For something to be misleading, it doesn't have to be untrue — you can easily make something sound really good or really bad, even if it isn't. You could use only some of the data rather than all of it, or only use statistics that support your point of view.

3) People who want to make a point sometimes present data in a biased way, e.g. governments who want to persuade voters, companies who want to sell their products, and environmental campaigners who want to persuade people to behave differently.

4) That's why all scientific evidence has to be looked at carefully to see if there any reasons for thinking the evidence (or the way it's presented) is biased in some way.

If Evidence Supports a Hypothesis, It's Accepted — for Now

1) If pretty much every scientist in the world believes a hypothesis to be true because experiments back it up, then it usually goes in the textbooks for students to learn.

Now we think it's more like this.

2) Our currently accepted theories are the ones that have survived this 'trial by evidence' — they've been tested many, many times over the years and survived (while the less good ones have been ditched).

3) However... they never, never become hard and fast, totally indisputable fact. You can never know... it'd only take one odd, totally inexplicable result, and the hypothesising and testing would start all over again.

4) There isn't a scientific answer to everything yet, not by a long way.

You expect me to believe that — then show me the evidence...

If scientists think something is true, they need to produce evidence to convince others — it's part of testing a hypothesis. Along the way some hypotheses will be disproved — shown not to be true. But if the hypothesis is correct then we've got a new explanation for something. It's how science works.

Correlation and Cause

Correlation and cause come up a lot in science. It's easy to get yourself into a mess of twisted logic, so read this page carefully and iron out anything you're not sure about right now.

A Correlation is a Relationship between two Factors

If there's a relationship between two things, then you can say there's a correlation between them, e.g.

- Sales of woolly hats increase when the weather is cold.
- Smoking increases your chances of getting lung cancer.
- A diet high in saturated fat increases your chances of developing high blood pressure.
- As pesticide use increases, the number of wild birds decreases.

A Correlation Doesn't Prove One Thing Causes Another

If you find a correlation between two things it's easy to think that one thing causes the other, but that's not always true — here's an example:

1) Primary school children with bigger feet tend to be better at maths. There's a correlation between the factor (big feet) and the outcome (better maths skills).

2) But it'd be crazy to say that having big feet causes you to be better at maths, (and even weirder to say that being good at maths causes bigger feet...).

3) There's another (hidden) factor involved — their age.

4) Older children are usually better at maths. They also usually have bigger feet. Age affects both their maths skills and the size of their feet.

5) If you really thought that there was a link between shoe size and ability at maths, you'd test this by comparing children of the same age — you have to control the other factors, so that the only factor that varies is foot size.

So all correlation means is that there's a link between a factor and an outcome. But even if there's a correlation between two factors, it doesn't always mean the outcome is inevitable — e.g. if you eat a diet high in saturated fat then it's more likely that you'll get heart disease, but it's not certain.

You've Got to do Valid Research

1) Scientists might have a hypothesis that there's a correlation between a factor and an outcome, and that one causes the other. They have to find evidence to support their hypothesis by doing a scientific study.

2) They have to consider all the other factors that might influence the outcome, and minimise the effects of these other factors (see p. 47 for more on this). They also need a large enough sample for any correlation to be meaningful.

3) Even if you've done your research and you've got evidence that a factor is correlated with an outcome, scientists don't usually accept the cause unless they can work out the mechanism that links the two things. E.g. smokers have an increased risk of lung cancer — the factor and the outcome are correlated. Cigarette smoke contains cancer-causing chemicals and it's inhaled into the lungs — this is the mechanism. So after a lot of research it's accepted that smoking can cause lung cancer.

4) Sometimes scientists show there's a correlation, but they can't find a mechanism to explain what's causing it. There might be a hidden factor influencing the results, or it could just be chance.

All sheep die — Elvis died, so he must have been a sheep...

You read about correlations in the media all the time and reporters often make the mistake of thinking that if two things are correlated then one must cause the other. Get into the habit of questioning what you read or hear, and thinking about whether it's just people jumping to conclusions about the cause.

How Science Works

Risk

By reading this page you are agreeing to the <u>risk</u> of a paper cut or severe drowsiness that could affect your ability to drive or operate heavy machinery... think carefully — the choice is yours.

Nothing is Risk-Free...

1) <u>Everything</u> that you do has a <u>risk</u> attached to it.

2) Scientists often identify risks — they show <u>correlations</u> between <u>factors</u> and <u>outcomes</u>.

3) Some risks seem pretty <u>obvious</u>, or we've known about them for a while, like the risk of getting <u>heart disease</u> if you're overweight, or of having a <u>car accident</u> when you're travelling in a car.

4) As <u>new technology</u> develops it can bring new risks, e.g. some scientists believe that using a mobile phone a lot may be <u>harmful</u>. There are lots of risks we <u>don't know about</u> yet.

5) There are <u>two main parts</u> to risk — the <u>chances</u> of something happening and how <u>serious</u> the <u>consequences</u> would be if it did. They usually add up to give an idea of how risky an activity is. So if something is <u>very likely</u> to happen and there are <u>serious consequences</u> it's <u>high-risk</u>.

People Make their Own Decisions about Risk...

1) Not all risks have the <u>same</u> level of <u>consequences</u> — if you use a sharp knife to chop vegetables, you risk cutting your finger. But if you go scuba-diving, you risk having a <u>fatal accident</u>.

2) There's much more <u>chance</u> of cutting your finger during <u>half an hour of chopping veg</u> than of dying in a diving accident during <u>half an hour of diving</u>. But people usually <u>accept</u> the high probability of an accident happening if the potential consequence is fairly <u>minor</u>, and not <u>long-lasting</u>.

3) People are also more willing to accept <u>high</u> levels of risk if they <u>enjoy</u> or <u>benefit</u> from the activity — for example car travel is quite <u>risky</u>, but the <u>convenience</u> of it means that people take the risk.

4) People's <u>perception</u> of risk (how risky they <u>think</u> something is) isn't always <u>accurate</u>. E.g. cycling on the roads can be <u>high-risk</u>. Many people are still <u>happy</u> to do it, because it's a <u>familiar</u> activity. Air travel is pretty safe, but people <u>perceive</u> it as a <u>high-risk</u> activity, and a lot of people are afraid of it.

5) The chances of something happening <u>increase</u> the more you do an activity — e.g. if you drive your car <u>every day</u>, but only fly <u>twice a year</u>, you're more likely to have a car crash than a plane crash.

6) There are different ways to assess the <u>size</u> of a risk. For example, you could look at the <u>number of people</u> struck by lightning each year per 10000 people, or at the chances of any <u>individual</u> being struck by lightning over the same time period.

We have to Choose Acceptable Levels of Risk...

1) People have to choose a <u>level</u> of risk that they find <u>acceptable</u>. This <u>varies</u> from person to person.

2) <u>Governments</u> and scientists often have to <u>choose</u> levels of risk in various situations on behalf of <u>other people</u>. They'll often be <u>influenced</u> by <u>public opinion</u> though.

3) <u>Reducing risk</u> can <u>cost</u> a lot, and it's <u>not possible</u> to <u>reduce</u> any risk to <u>zero</u>.

4) The people responsible aim to keep the risks <u>A</u>s <u>L</u>ow <u>A</u>s <u>R</u>easonably <u>A</u>chievable (the <u>ALARA</u> principle).

5) Many people react to risk using the <u>precautionary principle</u> (although they might not realise it...):

THE PRECAUTIONARY PRINCIPLE

If you're <u>not sure</u> about the possible results of doing something, and there's a <u>risk</u> of <u>serious</u> and <u>irreversible</u> harm, then it makes sense to <u>avoid</u> it, or to try to <u>reduce</u> the risk to a more <u>acceptable</u> level, e.g. by wearing a cycling helmet to protect you if you have an accident. Makes sense, really.

Take a risk — turn the page...

Risk isn't as <u>simple</u> as it looks — <u>risk management</u> is a really important job. It all boils down to maths in the end though — the <u>probability</u> of something happening and the <u>consequences</u> if it does. You can try to <u>reduce</u> the risk either by making it less likely to happen, or by making the consequences less severe.

Science Has Limits

Science can give us amazing things — cures for diseases, space travel, heated toilet seats...
But science has its limitations — there are questions that it just can't answer.

Some Questions Are Unanswered by Science — So Far

1) We don't understand everything. And we never will. We'll find out more, for sure — as more explanations are suggested and more experiments are done. But there'll always be stuff we don't know.

   For example, today we don't know as much as we'd like about climate change (global warming). Is climate change definitely happening? And to what extent is it caused by humans?

2) These are complicated questions. At the moment scientists don't all agree on the answers. But eventually, we probably will be able to answer these questions once and for all.

3) But by then there'll be loads of new questions to answer.

Other Questions Are Unanswerable by Science

1) Then there's the other type... questions that all the experiments in the world won't help us answer — the "Should we be doing this at all?" type questions. There are always two sides...

2) Take embryo screening (which allows you to choose an embryo with particular characteristics). It's possible to do it — but does that mean we should?

3) Different people have different opinions. For example...

   • Some people say it's good... couples whose existing child needs a bone marrow transplant, but who can't find a donor, will be able to have another child selected for its matching bone marrow. This would save the life of their first child — and if they want another child anyway... where's the harm?

   • Other people say it's bad... they say it could have serious effects on the child. In the above example the new child might feel unwanted — thinking they were only brought into the world to help someone else. And would they have the right to refuse to donate their bone marrow (as anyone else would)?

4) This question of whether something is morally or ethically right or wrong can't be answered by more experiments — there is no "right" or "wrong" answer.

5) The best we can do is get a consensus from society — a judgement that most people are more or less happy to live by. Science can provide more information to help people make this judgement, and the judgement might change over time. But in the end it's up to people and their conscience.

Loads of Other Factors Can Influence Decisions Too

Here are some other factors that can influence decisions about science, and the way science is used:

Economic factors:
   • Companies very often won't pay for research unless there's likely to be a profit in it.
   • Society can't always afford to do things scientists recommend without cutting back elsewhere (e.g. investing heavily in alternative energy sources).

Social factors:
   • Decisions based on scientific evidence affect people — e.g. should fossil fuels be taxed more highly (to invest in alternative energy)? Should alcohol be banned (to prevent health problems)? Would the effect on people's lifestyles be acceptable...

Environmental factors:
   • Genetically modified crops may help us produce more food — but some people say they could cause environmental problems.

Science doesn't have all the answers...

Nothing's ever simple, and science can only help you so far. It can tell you what's technically possible, but it's up to people to decide for themselves whether or not it's morally or ethically acceptable. Some people have extreme views on what we should or shouldn't do, and it can be hard to make decisions.

How Science Works

Genes, Chromosomes and DNA

Welcome to the first Biology bit of the OCR 21st Century Science Revision Guide. You're gonna love it.

1) Most cells in your body have a nucleus — and it's the nucleus that contains your genetic material.

2) The human cell nucleus contains 23 pairs of chromosomes. They're all well known and numbered. We all have two No. 19 chromosomes and two No. 12s, etc.

nucleus

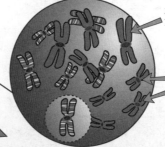

A single chromosome.

A pair of chromosomes. (They're always in pairs, one from each parent.)

3) Chromosomes carry genes. Different genes control the development of different characteristics, e.g. hair colour.

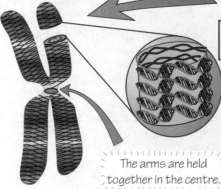

4) A gene is a short length of the chromosome...

DNA molecule

...which is one molecule of DNA.

The arms are held together in the centre.

5) The DNA is coiled up to form the arms of the chromosome.

6) Genes can exist in different versions. Each version gives a different characteristic, like blue or brown eyes. The different versions of the same gene are called alleles — see pages 7 and 8 for more information.

Genes are Instructions for Cells

Each gene is a code for making a certain protein. Proteins are the building blocks of cells. Having different versions of proteins means that we end up with different characteristics.

1) Some proteins are structural proteins. They're part of things like skin, hair, blood, and the cytoplasm in our cells.

2) Other proteins are enzymes. Enzymes control all the chemical reactions in an organism, e.g. respiration. Enzymes help with digestion by breaking down food molecules.

It's hard being a DNA molecule, there's so much to remember...

This is the top and bottom of genetics, so you definitely need to understand everything on this page or you'll find the rest of this topic dead hard. The best way to get all of these important facts engraved in your mind is to visit your local stone mason. Alternatively, cover the page, scribble down the main points and sketch out the diagrams... see how much you've remembered then learn the bits you missed.

Genes and Variation

Thought the fact that you haven't got your dad's <u>horrendous bushy eyebrows</u> was just a happy coincidence? There's a bit more to it...

Sperm and Egg Cells Have Half the Normal Amount of DNA

<u>Chromosomes</u> come in <u>pairs</u> because we have <u>two parents</u>.
One chromosome in every pair has come from each parent.

1) The <u>sex cells</u> (the sperm and the egg) are different from ordinary body cells because they contain just <u>23 single chromosomes</u>, instead of 23 pairs.

2) When the sperm <u>fertilises</u> the egg, the 23 chromosomes in the sperm combine with the 23 chromosomes in the egg.

3) The fertilised egg then has 23 <u>pairs</u> of chromosomes, just like an ordinary body cell.

4) The two chromosomes in a pair always carry the <u>same genes</u> and each gene is always found in the <u>same place</u> on the two chromosomes. Because the two chromosomes in a pair came from different parents, they might have different alleles of these genes. <u>Alleles</u> are different <u>versions</u> of the same gene.

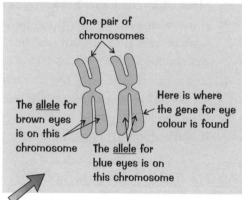

One pair of chromosomes

The <u>allele</u> for brown eyes is on this chromosome

Here is where the gene for eye colour is found

The <u>allele</u> for blue eyes is on this chromosome

Children Resemble Both Parents, But Are Identical to Neither

So, <u>half</u> a child's chromosomes have come from <u>each parent</u>. This means that —

1) Children get <u>some</u> of their alleles from <u>each</u> of their parents.

2) This is why most children look a bit like <u>both</u> of their parents.

3) But they won't be <u>exactly</u> like either one of their parents because they haven't got <u>all</u> the same alleles — some came from the <u>other</u> parent.

4) In fact, every child will have a new, <u>unique</u>, combination of alleles — that's why no two people in the world are exactly the same (apart from identical twins, but you don't need to worry about that til p11).

Genes Are Shuffled Together Randomly to Make Eggs and Sperm

When people <u>produce sperm</u> or <u>egg</u> cells, their pairs of chromosomes <u>separate</u> and go into different cells.

1) The two chromosomes in a pair are <u>never identical</u> because they have <u>different alleles</u>.

2) So, when they go into two different sex cells, each of the two cells gets <u>different alleles</u>.

3) Each of the 23 chromosome pairs separates <u>independently</u>.

4) So there are <u>millions</u> of different <u>chromosome combinations</u> that can be produced from the separation of 23 pairs. (Actually, about 8 million different combinations.)

So a sex cell could end up with version one of chromosome one, but version two of chromosomes two and three, etc.

5) This means that all the <u>sex cells</u> produced by one individual will probably all be <u>genetically different</u>. When a woman releases an egg it can be fertilised by <u>any one</u> of millions of different sperm released by her partner.

6) All of this means that the chances of two siblings being identical are <u>absolutely minuscule</u>. Brothers and sisters tend to look a bit alike, but there are <u>always differences</u>.

Genes — they always come in pairs...

So, a mixture of chromosomes are <u>randomly shuffled</u> up as they go into the sex cells. Then a random sex cell fuses with another <u>random</u> sex cell at <u>fertilisation</u> (oh, the romance of it all).

Inheritance

In genetics you're never more than a stone's throw away from a genetic diagram.

Genetic Diagrams Show the Possible Alleles of Offspring

1) As I keep saying, alleles are different versions of the same gene.

2) Most of the time you have two of each gene (i.e. two alleles) — one from each parent.

3) If the alleles are different you have instructions for two different versions of a characteristic (e.g. blue eyes or brown eyes), but you only develop one version of the two (e.g. brown eyes). The version of the characteristic that appears is caused by the dominant allele. The other allele is said to be recessive.

4) In genetic diagrams, letters are used to represent alleles. Alleles that produce dominant characteristics are always shown with a capital letter, and alleles that produce recessive characteristics with a small letter.

5) If you're homozygous for a trait, you have two alleles the same for that particular gene, e.g. CC or cc. If you're heterozygous for a trait, you have two different alleles for that particular gene, e.g. Cc.

You Need to Interpret, Explain and Construct Genetic Diagrams

Imagine you're cross-breeding hamsters, and that some have a normal, boring disposition while others have a leaning towards crazy acrobatics. And suppose you know the behaviour is due to one gene...

Let's say that the allele which causes the crazy nature is recessive — so use a 'b'.
And normal (boring) behaviour is due to a dominant allele — call it 'B'.

1) For an organism to display a recessive characteristic, both its alleles must be recessive — so a crazy hamster must have the alleles 'bb' (i.e. it must be homozygous for this trait).

2) However, a normal hamster could be BB (homozygous) or Bb (heterozygous), because the dominant allele (B) overrules the recessive one (b).

So if you cross a crazy hamster, genetic type bb, with a homozygous normal hamster, BB, you get this...

Parents: normal and boring parent   crazy parent

Parents' alleles: **BB**   **bb**

Alleles in eggs and sperm: **B**   **B**   **b**   **b**

Possible combinations of alleles in offspring: **Bb**   **Bb**   **Bb**   **Bb**

They're all normal and boring.

The lines show all the possible ways the parents' alleles could combine.

Remember, only one of these possibilities would actually happen for any one offspring.

If two of these offspring now breed they will produce new combinations of alleles in their kids.

This time, there's a 75% chance of having a normal boring hamster and a 25% chance of a crazy one.

Parents: normal and boring   normal and boring

Parents' alleles: **Bb**   **Bb**

Alleles in eggs and sperm: **B**   **b**   **B**   **b**

Possible combinations of alleles in offspring: **BB**   **Bb**   **Bb**   **bb**

normal   normal   normal   crazy!

It's not just hamsters that have the wild and scratty allele...

...my sister definitely has it too. Remember, 'results' like this are only probabilities. It doesn't mean it'll actually happen. (Most likely, you'll end up trying to contain a mini-riot of nine lunatic baby hamsters.)

Girl or Boy?

It's pretty easy to tell the difference between boys and girls, but the way it works genetically is slightly more complex.

Your Chromosomes Control Whether You're Male or Female

There are 23 pairs of chromosomes in every human body cell. The 23rd pair are labelled XY.

These are sex chromosomes — they decide whether you turn out male or female.

> All men have an X and a Y chromosome: XY
> The Y chromosome causes male characteristics.

> All women have two X chromosomes: XX
> The lack of a Y chromosome causes female characteristics.

Like all other characteristics, sex is determined by a gene. The Y chromosome carries a gene which makes an embryo develop into a male as it grows. Females, who always have two X chromosomes, don't have this gene and so they develop in a different way.

There's an Equal Chance of Having a Boy or a Girl...

...and here's a genetic diagram to prove it.

1) The genetic diagram for sex inheritance is fairly similar to a bog-standard one. It just shows the sex chromosomes rather than different alleles.

2) When you plug all the letters into the diagram, it shows that there are two XX results and two XY results, so there's the same probability of getting a boy or a girl.

3) Don't forget that this 50:50 ratio is only a probability. If you had four kids they could all be boys. Eeeuch.

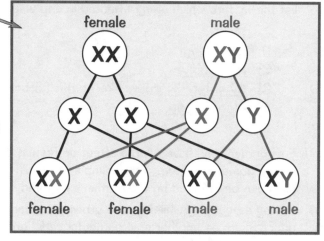

One Gene Determines Which Sex Organs You Develop

One little gene causes some fairly major changes...

1) The gene that makes an embryo into a male causes a protein called testis determining factor (TDF) to be produced.

2) When the embryo's reproductive system begins to develop, TDF causes the development of testes (instead of ovaries).

3) The testes then produce male sex hormones, which in turn make the rest of the male reproductive system develop.

4) In females there's no TDF and so the embryo develops ovaries and the rest of a female reproductive system.

I thought it was all to do with crisps and cereal...

I have a theory that the two big differences between boys and girls are that boys eat crisps more than one at a time and they mix different types of cereal together in the same bowl.

Inheritance and Environment

This page is all about why different individuals from the same species <u>look</u> or <u>behave</u> slightly differently from each other. You know, a bit taller or a bit fatter or a bit more scary-to-look-at, etc. There are two things that create these differences — <u>genes</u> and the <u>environment</u>.

Characteristics <u>Usually</u> <u>Depend on</u> <u>Combinations</u> <u>of Genes</u>

1) The example you saw on the last page was controlled by <u>just one gene</u>, but don't go thinking this is the way <u>all</u> characteristics are controlled.

2) It's actually quite <u>rare</u> for a characteristic to depend on just a single gene.

3) Usually, there are <u>lots</u> of different genes, and these all <u>work together</u> to determine a characteristic.

4) This makes inheritance very <u>unpredictable</u> — because the genes all interact, and there are hundreds, or even thousands, of different possible <u>combinations</u> of alleles.

5) For example, <u>height</u> is determined by a combination of genes.

The <u>Environment</u> <u>Affects</u> <u>Nearly Every</u> <u>Characteristic</u>

1) Most variation in animals is caused by a <u>mixture</u> of <u>genetic</u> and <u>environmental</u> factors.

2) Almost every single aspect of a human (or other organism) is <u>affected by</u> <u>our environment</u> in some way, however small. In fact it's a lot <u>easier</u> to list the factors which <u>aren't</u> affected in any way by environment:

> If you're not sure what "environment" means, think of it as "upbringing" instead.

    1) <u>Eye colour</u>
    2) <u>Hair colour</u>
    3) <u>Inherited disorders</u> like cystic fibrosis etc.
    4) <u>Blood group</u>

3) <u>Environment</u> can have a large effect on human growth even <u>before</u> someone's born. For example, a baby's <u>weight</u> at birth can be affected by the mother's <u>diet</u> and <u>lifestyle</u>.

4) Having a <u>poor diet</u> whilst you're growing up can also <u>stunt</u> <u>your growth</u> — another environmental variation.

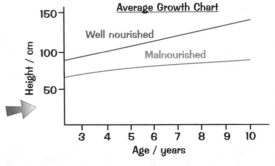

5) For some characteristics, it's hard to say which factor is more important — genes or environment...

HEALTH — Some people are more likely to get certain <u>diseases</u> (e.g. <u>cancer</u> and <u>heart disease</u>) because of their genes. But <u>lifestyle</u> also affects the risk, e.g. if you smoke or only eat junk food you're more likely to get ill.

INTELLIGENCE — One theory is that although your <u>maximum possible IQ</u> might be determined by your <u>genes</u>, whether you get to it depends on your <u>environment</u>, e.g. your <u>upbringing</u>, <u>school</u> life and <u>diet</u>.

SPORTING ABILITY — Genes determine your <u>potential</u>, but training is important too.

Revision? I'm relying on my genetic ability...

Somehow, I doubt that you've <u>inherited</u> an encyclopedic knowledge of OCR 21st Century Science from your parents, so you'd best hedge your bets and do some revision. Whilst you're at it make sure that the <u>environmental</u> factors don't let you down — you'll need plenty of <u>coffee</u> and <u>chocolate</u>.

Clones

Cloning seems to be a hot topic in the news at the moment but nature has been making clones for millions of years and nobody seems that bothered.

Clones Are Genetically Identical Organisms

1) Sexual reproduction produces offspring that are genetically different. But other methods of reproduction can produce offspring that are genetically identical to each other.

2) Genetically identical organisms are called clones. Clones have the same genes, and also the same alleles of those genes.

3) Because clones have the same alleles, any differences between them must be due to differences in their environment — for example, the amount of food available.

Nature Makes Clones...

(i) By Asexual Reproduction

Some organisms reproduce asexually (without sexual reproduction). This means that there is only one parent, and the offspring are genetically the same as each other and the parent.

1) Most bacteria reproduce like this — they simply divide into two. This means they can multiply very quickly.

2) Many plants can also reproduce asexually. They produce an offshoot, which develops as a separate plant.

Pollination of flowers is sexual reproduction and it produces genetically different offspring. Some plants can do both types of reproduction.

3) A few animals can reproduce asexually. Female greenfly don't need to mate — they can just lay eggs, which develop into more females. They can also reproduce sexually, when the mood takes them.

(ii) When Cells of an Embryo Split

Identical twins are also clones.

1) A single egg is fertilised by a sperm, and an embryo begins to develop as normal.

2) Occasionally, the embryo splits into two, and two separate embryos begin to develop.

3) The two embryos are genetically identical. So, two genetically identical babies are born.

Scientists Can Now Make Clones in the Lab

Nowadays, clones can also be made by scientists in the lab:

1) The nucleus of an egg cell is removed (to form an enucleated cell) — this leaves the egg cell without any genetic information.

2) A nucleus from an adult donor cell is inserted in its place.

3) The cell is then stimulated so that it starts dividing as if it was a normal embryo (fertilised egg).

4) The embryo produced is genetically identical to the donor cell.

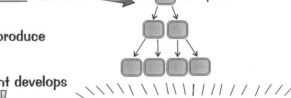

An evil dictator might make an army of clones to rule the Galaxy...

That might be a good idea for a film, come to think of it. Make sure you know the ways that clones are produced naturally and the way they can be produced artificially by scientists. So, learn everything on the page, cover it up and see if you can clone it onto a blank piece of paper.

Genetic Disorders

Unfortunately, some genes can cause nasty diseases.

Genetic Disorders Are Caused by Faulty Alleles

1) Some <u>diseases</u> are <u>inherited</u> — one or both parents carry a <u>faulty allele</u> and pass it on to their children.

2) <u>Cystic fibrosis</u> and <u>Huntington's disorder</u> are both caused by a faulty allele of a <u>single gene</u>.

Some Genetic Disorders Are Caused by Recessive Alleles...

<u>Defective alleles</u> are responsible for <u>genetic disorders</u>. Most of these defective alleles are <u>recessive</u>.
<u>Cystic fibrosis</u> is a <u>genetic disorder</u> of the <u>cell membranes</u>. It <u>results</u> in the body producing a lot
of thick, sticky <u>mucus</u> in the <u>air passages</u>, <u>gut</u> and <u>pancreas</u>.

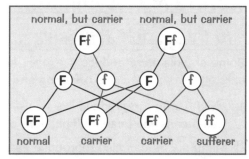

1) The allele which causes cystic fibrosis is a <u>recessive allele</u>,
    'f', carried by about <u>1 person in 25</u>.

2) Because it's recessive, people with only <u>one copy</u> of the
    allele <u>won't</u> have the disorder — they're known as <u>carriers</u>.

3) For a child to have a chance of inheriting the disorder, <u>both</u>
    <u>parents</u> must be either <u>carriers</u> or <u>sufferers</u>.

4) As the diagram shows, there's a <u>1 in 4 chance</u> of a child
    having the disorder if <u>both</u> parents are <u>carriers</u>.

Knowing how inheritance works can help you to interpret a <u>family tree</u> — this is one for <u>cystic fibrosis</u>.

1) From the family tree, you can tell that the allele for
    cystic fibrosis <u>isn't</u> dominant because plenty of
    the family <u>carry</u> the allele but <u>aren't sufferers</u>.

2) There is a <u>25%</u> chance that the new baby will
    be a sufferer and a <u>50%</u> chance that it will be
    a carrier because both of its parents are
    carriers but not sufferers. The case of the new
    baby is just the same as in the genetic diagram
    further up the page — so the baby could be
    <u>normal</u> (FF), a <u>carrier</u> (Ff) or a <u>sufferer</u> (ff).

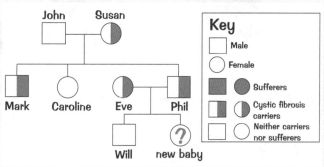

Others Are Caused by Dominant Alleles...

1) Unlike cystic fibrosis, <u>Huntington's disorder</u>
    is caused by a <u>dominant</u> allele.

2) The disorder causes <u>shaking</u>, <u>erratic body movements</u>
    and <u>mental deterioration</u> and there's <u>no cure</u>.

3) The dominant allele means there's a <u>50%</u> chance
    of each child inheriting the disorder if just one parent
    is a carrier. These are seriously grim odds.

4) The "carrier" parent will of course be a <u>sufferer</u> too since the
    allele is dominant, but the symptoms do not appear until after
    the age of 40, by which time the allele has been <u>passed on</u> to
    children and even grandchildren. Hence the disorder persists.

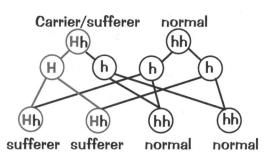

So, if one parent is a sufferer, there's
a 1 in 2 chance of each of their
children having the disorder.

Unintentional mooning — caused by faulty genes...

We <u>all</u> have defective genes in us somewhere — but usually they don't cause us a problem (as they're
often <u>recessive</u>, so if you have a healthy <u>dominant</u> allele too, you'll be fine). At the moment scientists
are looking at new ways of treating genetic disorders using <u>gene therapy</u>, which is covered on page 14.

Genetic Testing

Nowadays it's possible to test for all sorts of different genetic conditions, but this has thrown up some pretty big questions about what we should and shouldn't be doing.

Embryos Can Be Screened for Some Disorders

1) When embryos are produced using IVF (that's *in vitro* fertilisation or test-tube babies), doctors can test the embryos to check if they've got any genetic disorders. This is called genetic screening. This is especially important if there's concern that one of the parents might carry alleles for a genetic disorder.

2) Often doctors produce more embryos than they need during IVF. When this happens all the embryos get screened and only healthy ones are chosen to be implanted into the mother's womb.

3) This process is known as pre-implantation genetic diagnosis.

Genetic Testing Can Lead to Some Hard Choices

It's also possible to do genetic tests without IVF.

1) People can have a test to see if they will develop Huntington's disorder when they get older. People who know they have Huntington's disorder might choose not to have children.

2) Adults can be checked to see if they carry alleles for genetic disorders. If a couple find out that their children might inherit a genetic disorder, then they might decide not to have children.

3) A developing fetus in the womb can also be checked. If it turns out that the fetus has a serious genetic disorder, the parents might decide to have a termination (abortion).

Even if We Can Do Something... It Might Be Best if We Don't

Science has made it possible to do these things, but scientists can't say whether we should do them. That's for individuals or society to decide. Some of the issues with genetic testing are:

RELIABILITY

No genetic tests are 100% accurate. There are always some errors due to things like samples getting contaminated or misinterpretation of results. This means people have to make decisions based on information that may be incorrect.

SAFETY

Like most medical procedures, tests carried out during pregnancy aren't 100% safe. Amniocentesis (testing the fluid surrounding the fetus), which is used to detect cystic fibrosis and Down's syndrome, causes a miscarriage in 0.5 to 1% of cases.

When tests are carried out, there can be more decisions to make once the results have arrived. E.g.

1) If a test result is positive, should other members of a family be tested? Some people may prefer not to know, but is this fair on any partners or future children they might have?

2) Is it right for someone who's at risk of passing on a genetic condition to have children? Is it fair to put them under pressure not to, if they decide they want children?

3) If a test carried out during a pregnancy is positive, is it right to terminate the pregnancy? Perhaps the parents wouldn't be able to cope with a sick or disabled child, but does that child have less right to life than a healthy child? Some people think abortion is always wrong, whatever the circumstances.

Get ready for some genetic testing in the exam...

This is one of the really big topics so chances are it'll crop up somewhere in one of your exams. You need to understand what genetic testing is and when it is used. You also need to be clued up on the ethical issues — be aware of all the pros and cons, not just your own opinion.

Gene Therapy and Ethics

Gene therapy is a new science with exciting possibilities. There are hopes that it could really help people with genetic disorders like cystic fibrosis. But, like other areas of genetics, there are concerns that it may lead to some pretty serious problems...

Gene Therapy Could Improve Lives...

Gene therapy may soon make it possible to treat or prevent genetic disorders by correcting faulty genes.

Example 1 — Treating Cystic Fibrosis

1) Cystic fibrosis (CF) affects about 1 in 2500 people in the UK.

2) Scientists are trying to treat cystic fibrosis with gene therapy. One method being tried out is the use of a virus to insert a healthy copy of the gene into cells in the airways.

3) There are some problems — for example, at the moment the effect wears off after a few days. But there are big hopes that gene therapy will one day mean CF can be treated effectively.

Example 2 — Preventing Breast Cancer

1) Breast cancer is a disease where cells grow uncontrollably, causing tumours. Some people inherit defective genes that predispose them to getting breast cancer.

2) In theory it's possible to supplement the faulty genes with working, healthy ones using gene therapy — this would have to be done before a tumour grows.

3) Scientists can't do this yet because they need to identify the genes involved (there's more than one), and they need to target the working genes to the breast area.

4) But not all breast cancers are caused by faulty genes — so giving someone the working gene will mean they're no longer predisposed, but they could still get breast cancer anyway.

...Or it Could be Misused

Being able to prevent and treat diseases sounds great, but there are some potential drawbacks —

1) People would have to have their genes analysed which can have certain risks (see page 13).

2) If an unborn baby is found to carry faulty genes, the parents might think about an abortion, which as you probably know is a pretty controversial issue itself.

3) People who find out that they are carriers of faulty alleles may become depressed.

4) If the information becomes available to others, this might cause discrimination. Employers might not want to give a job to someone who is likely to get ill. However, some people argue that employers would be able to use the results of genetic tests to make sure that they don't expose their employees to anything that might be especially dangerous to them because of the genes they have.

5) Insurance companies might refuse to give life insurance to people with the "wrong" alleles.

6) Gene therapies carry risks themselves — they might affect other cells besides the target cells. There are concerns that they could even cause cancers instead of preventing them.

Gene therapy — talk things through with your Levi's...

Gene therapy is another ethical minefield. It throws up all sorts of questions, including exactly what should be classed as a 'disease' that needs fixing. Many people would argue that treating cystic fibrosis is a good thing, but what about high blood pressure, or an inability to tan... where does it stop?

Stem Cells

Stem cell research has <u>exciting possibilities</u> too, but it's also pretty <u>controversial</u>.

Stem Cells Can Become ANY Type of Cell

1) Most cells in your body are <u>specialised</u> for a particular job. E.g. white blood cells are brilliant at fighting invaders, but they can't carry oxygen like red blood cells.

2) <u>Differentiation</u> is the process by which a cell <u>changes</u> to become <u>specialised</u> for its job. In most <u>animal</u> cells, the ability to differentiate is <u>lost</u> at an early stage.

3) Some cells are <u>undifferentiated</u>. They can develop into <u>different types of cell</u> depending on what <u>instructions</u> they're given. These cells are called <u>STEM CELLS</u>.

4) Stem cells are found in early human <u>embryos</u>. They're <u>exciting</u> to doctors and medical researchers because they have the potential to turn into <u>any</u> kind of cell at all. This makes sense if you think about it — <u>all</u> the <u>different types</u> of cell found in a human being have to come from those <u>few cells</u> in the early embryo.

undifferentiated stem cell → differentiated white blood cell

Stem Cells May Be Able to Cure Many Diseases

1) Medicine <u>already</u> uses adult stem cells to cure <u>disease</u>. For example, people with some <u>blood diseases</u> (e.g. <u>sickle cell anaemia</u>) can be treated by <u>bone marrow transplants</u>. Bone marrow contains <u>stem cells</u> that can turn into <u>new blood cells</u> to replace the faulty old ones.

2) Scientists can also <u>extract</u> stem cells from very early human <u>embryos</u> and <u>grow</u> them.

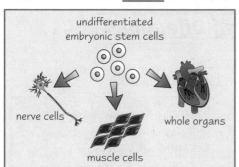

undifferentiated embryonic stem cells

nerve cells

muscle cells

whole organs

3) These embryonic stem cells could be used to <u>replace faulty cells</u> in sick people — you could make <u>beating heart muscle cells</u> for people with <u>heart disease</u>, <u>insulin-producing cells</u> for people with <u>diabetes</u>, <u>nerve cells</u> for people <u>paralysed by spinal injuries</u>, and so on.

4) To get cultures of <u>one specific type</u> of cell, researchers try to <u>control</u> the differentiation of the stem cells by changing the environment they're growing in. So far, it's still a bit hit and miss — lots more <u>research</u> is needed.

One way that stem cell treatment might work is by making an <u>embryo</u> that's a <u>clone</u> of a patient with an illness. Stem cells could then be extracted from the embryo and <u>implanted</u> into the patient to treat their illness. The big advantage of this is that the stem cells would be <u>genetically</u> identical to the patient and so their body <u>wouldn't reject</u> them.

The Use of Stem Cells Is Controversial

There are lots of arguments <u>for</u> and <u>against</u> the use of stem cells from embryos:

In favour of using stem cells from embryos	Against using stem cells from embryos
Early human embryos are only balls of cells – they are not yet human beings with rights.	These new "cures" are still unproven. Research may be carried out which turns out to be useless, causing the unnecessary deaths of many embryos.
The needs of an adult or a child with a crippling disease are more important than the needs of an unborn embryo.	It's especially important to protect the rights of the unborn, because they can't speak up for themselves.
Research using a few embryos might bring benefits to thousands of people.	Killing human life is wrong, whatever the circumstances.
	Only God should have the power to create and destroy life.

My brother played God in a school play... I was Mary

Many people have very passionate views about stem cell research. So far, the only time <u>George Bush</u> has ever <u>vetoed</u> (banned) a law was to prevent a law allowing <u>stem cell research</u> using <u>frozen embryos</u>.

Science and Ethics

Genetics can be even more controversial than when Harold Bishop came back from the dead in Neighbours.

Scientific Advances Usually Have Benefits and Costs

Scientists have created loads of new technologies that could improve our lives.
In genetics, for example, benefits include:

1) Allowing infertile couples to use IVF to have babies.
2) Being able to identify whether a fetus has a genetic disorder.
3) Identifying whether an adult is likely to get a disease, such as cancer later, in life.
4) Growth of human (or animal) cells to be used as spare parts, for example in transplant surgery.
5) The possibility of being able to insert healthy alleles into the cells of people with genetic disorders.

However, it's not all good news. Some of the costs are —

1) Scientific research is expensive and uncertain. Perhaps the money that goes into research would be better spent on things like building new hospitals and training doctors.
2) No one knows what the results of genetic experiments will be, which is risky. Who knows what might happen if scientists alter the pattern of our DNA?
3) Some people think that using stem cells from human embryos is an unacceptable cost.

There are many different opinions about whether or not the benefits outweigh the costs...

There Are Two Key Approaches to Ethical Dilemmas

Of course, there are many different ways of looking at ethical dilemmas.
For the exam you need to be able to develop arguments based on two key principles:

1) You may think that certain actions are always unnatural or wrong. This means that, whatever the possible benefits, you feel these actions are unacceptable. Some people would say that research on human embryos comes into this category.

2) You may also say that the right decision is the one that brings the greatest benefit to the greatest number of people. Some people would argue that embryo research does more good than harm and so it is acceptable.

Another consideration is that some people think it's unfair for people to benefit from something which is only possible because someone else has suffered or taken a risk. The trouble is, all new medicines and medical procedures must be tested on human volunteers — and that always involves some risk.

The Law is Sometimes Involved Too

As well as individuals, the law is involved in regulating scientific research.

1) Animal research is regulated. For example, in the UK, scientists researching on vertebrates must have a licence and they must show that the likely benefits of the research outweigh the animals' suffering.
2) No research is allowed on embryos older than 14 days.
3) Genetic manipulation is also regulated. In Britain, genetic manipulation of human body cells is allowed, but the modification of reproductive cells (sperm and egg cells) isn't.
4) There are regulations about the effect of research on the environment, e.g. pollution is monitored.

Hmmm, tricky...

As you can see, this unit isn't just about knowing your facts — you need to think about the ethical issues in genetics and the kinds of arguments people consider to make decisions about what should be done.

Revision Summary for Module B1

Well done, you've made it to the end of the first section of the book — only nine more to go. I know you're chomping at the bit to move onto C1, but you ain't quite finished here yet. Have a go at all of these questions and see how many you can get right. Then go back through the section and learn the bits you got stuck on. If you can do all of them without looking then you'll be onto a winner for the exam.

1) Where is DNA found within a cell?

2) True or false — chromosomes are usually found in groups of four?

3) What is a gene?

4) Why are genes so important?

5) What are alleles?

6) Name the two types of sex cell.

7) Why do most children look a bit like both of their parents but not identical to either?

8)* Why is it virtually impossible for two people who aren't identical twins to have the same DNA?

9) Do you need a licence to keep flamingos in the UK?

10) What's the difference between homozygous and heterozygous?

11)* Draw a genetic diagram for the possible inheritance of an allele for loving Lemar albums. The allele is dominant and one parent is homozygous (LL) and one is heterozygous (Ll).

12) What does TDF stand for?

13) What's the difference between males and females in terms of their chromosomes?

14) Name a characteristic that is determined by genes alone.

15) Is height determined by genes, the environment or both?

16) True or false — most scientists believe intelligence is determined by the environment alone?

17) Write a definition of the term 'clone'.

18) How can some species of the following reproduce asexually: bacteria, plants and animals?

19) How are identical twins formed?

20) What is an enucleated cell?

21) Is the allele for cystic fibrosis dominant or recessive?

22) What are the symptoms of cystic fibrosis?

23) What are the symptoms of Huntington's disorder?

24) What is the chance of a child inheriting Huntington's disorder if one of their parents is a carrier?

25) Why are embryos screened during IVF treatment?

26) What are the two main problems with genetic screening?

27) Name two diseases that may be treated using gene therapy in the future.

28) What is differentiation?

29) What advantage would treating patients with stem cells taken from their own cloned embryos have?

30) List some ethical arguments for and against using stem cells from embryos.

31) Give some examples of laws that regulate scientific research.

* Answers on page 104.

Chemicals From The Earth

Funny isn't it — you've been breathing in, breathing out, walking on, eating, playing with and generally using tons of <u>chemicals</u> for the last sixteen or so years of your life. But how many can you name, eh?

The <u>Atmosphere</u> Contains <u>Various</u> Chemicals

1) The Earth is surrounded by an <u>atmosphere</u> made up mainly of <u>nitrogen</u>, <u>oxygen</u> and <u>argon</u>, plus small amounts of <u>water vapour</u>, <u>carbon dioxide</u>, and other <u>gases</u>.

2) The relative <u>proportions</u> of gases in the atmosphere are about:

> Nitrogen 78%
> Oxygen 21%
> Argon 1%

These figures are rounded up slightly, which explains how there's room for water vapour, carbon dioxide etc. too.

Here's a picture of the <u>Earth</u> from space.

The blue haze around the Earth is its <u>atmosphere</u>.

SCIENCE PHOTO LIBRARY

Hydrocarbons are Massively Important Chemicals

The majority of <u>fuels</u> contain just two elements — <u>carbon</u> and <u>hydrogen</u>. These are known as <u>hydrocarbons</u>, and they all come from <u>crude oil</u>, which is drilled out of the <u>Earth</u>.

> 1) Fuels such as <u>petrol</u>, <u>diesel fuel</u> and <u>fuel oil</u> are all mixtures of <u>hydrocarbons</u>.
> 2) A hydrocarbon is a <u>compound</u> of <u>hydrogen</u> and <u>carbon</u> — fairly simple.
> 3) The only <u>difference</u> between different fuels (petrol, diesel and fuel oil, for example) is the <u>size</u> of the hydrocarbons they contain.

Hydrocarbons are also known as <u>fossil fuels</u>.

<u>Coal</u> is a fuel that's different — it's mainly made of only <u>one element</u> — <u>carbon</u>. Here are some very simple diagrams to show the basic structure of <u>hydrocarbons</u>.

 = carbon atom   = hydrogen atom

The only difference between these two fuels is the length of the hydrocarbon chains.

HYDROCARBON SUCH AS PETROL

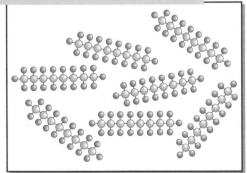

HYDROCARBON SUCH AS DIESEL

Chemistry — what an atomic subject...

This section's got some lovely pretty diagrams of chemicals. Look at those nice pastel colours — I chose them specially so they'd not scare you too much. Think about these <u>chemical</u> things as little <u>atom-blobs</u> joined to each other, all just chilling in a happy pastel world. Ahhh, it's all going to be OK.

Chemical Reactions: Combustion

Combustion is just a posh word for burning. But that's not all you need to know...

Atoms are Rearranged When a Hydrocarbon Burns

1) When fuels burn, the hydrogen atoms in the fuel combine with oxygen from the air to make hydrogen oxide (otherwise known as water).

2) The carbon atoms in the fuel combine with oxygen from the air to make carbon dioxide.

3) Hydrocarbons are made of both hydrogen and carbon atoms, which means that both water and carbon dioxide are produced when hydrocarbons burn.

4) Another way of describing this reaction is by saying that hydrogen, carbon and oxygen atoms from both the hydrocarbon and the air all rearrange themselves into carbon dioxide and water.

5) The posh name for this rearrangement is COMBUSTION.
Here's a diagram of hydrocarbon combustion:

 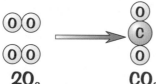 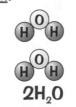

CH_4 $2O_2$ CO_2 $2H_2O$

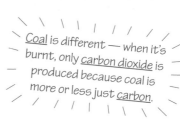
Coal is different — when it's burnt, only carbon dioxide is produced because coal is more or less just carbon.

Chemical Reactions Happen When Atoms are Rearranged

You've just found out about the way atoms rearrange themselves when fuels burn.
These sorts of rearrangements happen everywhere in chemistry — in every chemical reaction.
Don't panic yet — chemical reactions are really straightforward. They're just when atoms change places.

1) When a chemical reaction happens, the atoms rearrange themselves into new substances.

Substance A   Substance B   Substance C

      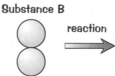   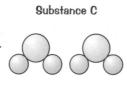
reaction

After the reaction, the atoms are still there, but have rearranged themselves into different chemicals.

2) Here's an example of a real chemical reaction:

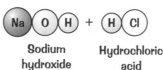   reaction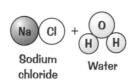

Sodium hydroxide   Hydrochloric acid   Sodium chloride   Water

3) These rearrangements can be represented by symbol equations. The atoms before and after the reaction are represented by symbols (letters), and numbers show how many of each thing there are. For example, here's the burning of magnesium:

 +   reaction

Magnesium   Oxygen   Magnesium Oxide

And here's the symbol equation of this reaction:

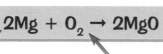
$$2Mg + O_2 \rightarrow 2MgO$$

The big number, (the 2 in 2Mg), tells you that there are 2 atoms of Mg.

The little number, (the 2 in O_2), tells you that there are 2 atoms of O in one molecule of it. Look at the diagram for help.

The one burning question is... have you learnt it all...?

So when stuff burns, or when some other sort of chemical reaction happens, the atoms split apart and then join up with different atoms. You can then write down what happens with numbers and letters saying how many of each type of substance there is. It can seem confusing, but I'm sure you'll get it.

Fuels and Pollutants

Now you're going to learn about the products of reactions, and how some of them are polluting and nasty.

Reactants and Products Contain the Same Atoms...

Remember this — atoms don't just appear or vanish during a chemical reaction.

The atoms in the chemicals before the reaction (the reactants) are still present in the chemicals after the reaction (the products). For example, here's the reaction of sodium and chlorine:

$$2Na + Cl_2 \rightarrow 2NaCl \text{ (sodium + chlorine} \rightarrow \text{sodium chloride)}$$

Before reaction (reactants)   After reaction (products)

(Na) (Na) + (Cl Cl) → (Na Cl)

2 sodium   2 chlorine   (Na Cl)
atoms   atoms   2 chlorine atoms
                                                  and 2 sodium atoms

The products and reactants have exactly the same atoms — they're just arranged differently.

...But Can Have Very Different Properties

Reactants and products contain the same atoms, but they don't have the same properties.

1) Once the atoms have rearranged in a reaction, the new compounds have their own properties.

2) The properties of the products can be very different to the properties of the reactants.

3) The sodium and chlorine reaction is a good example. Sodium is so dangerous that it will burn you if you touch it, and chlorine is a poisonous gas. When these two horrible chemicals react together, you get sodium chloride — also known as edible table salt.

Tasty salt has exactly the same atoms as a poisonous gas and something that burns your skin. Amazing.

Air Pollution can be Caused by Products of Combustion

As you saw on the last page, when a fuel burns the atoms in the fuel and the oxygen atoms in the air rearrange themselves into new chemicals.

1) These new chemicals have to go somewhere — usually the atmosphere.

2) This is a problem because these chemicals aren't always good for us or the environment.

3) Chemicals produced by burning fuels that are harmful to us or the environment are called pollutants.

4) Some pollutants are toxic — they can directly cause disease or death if breathed in over a long period of time. For example, there is evidence that air pollution contributes to disorders such as asthma.

5) Pollutants can also harm us indirectly. For example, there is evidence that some pollutants cause acid rain which can make it difficult for us to grow food. Pollutants also contribute to the greenhouse effect, which is causing the Earth to warm up very slowly.

Stop being so reactive... it's only chemistry...

We burn fuels all the time to heat our houses and run our cars, so we're constantly filling the air with pollutants. The atmosphere is overflowing with carbon dioxide as a result, causing the polar ice caps to melt, the world's climate to change, and everything to generally go wrong. It's depressing reading...

Pollution: Carbon

Here's another page on all the bad things that happen when you burn fossil fuels. It's all bad bad bad.

Different Forms of Carbon Pollution Cause Different Problems

Fossils fuels are burnt to produce energy. We burn fossil fuels to power vehicles and to produce electricity in power stations. The carbon-based products of burning fossil fuels often pollute the atmosphere.

1) All fossils fuels contain large amounts of the element carbon, so it's no surprise that these fuels produce a lot of pollutants that contain carbon.

2) If the fuel is burnt where there's lots of oxygen available, then carbon dioxide is produced. This adds to the carbon dioxide that's found naturally in the atmosphere.

3) If there's not much oxygen available, such as in a car engine, then small amounts of carbon monoxide and small particles of carbon are produced instead.

4) Carbon dioxide, carbon monoxide and carbon particles are all pollutants.

Carbon Dioxide

1) Carbon dioxide has the formula CO_2, which means that a molecule of carbon dioxide has two oxygen atoms joined to one carbon atom.

2) In the same way, water's formula, H_2O, tells us that a molecule of water is made of two hydrogen atoms joined to one oxygen atom.

3) Carbon dioxide (CO_2), like any other pollutant, will stay in the atmosphere causing problems until it's removed.

4) CO_2 can be removed from the atmosphere naturally. Plants use up CO_2 from the air when they photosynthesise. CO_2 also dissolves in rainwater and in seas, lakes and rivers.

5) Despite these ways of removing CO_2 from the atmosphere, CO_2 levels will still increase if human activity, like burning fuels, adds extra CO_2 into the atmosphere.

6) Increased CO_2 levels cause the greenhouse effect, which is warming up the Earth. This may change the world's climate and weather patterns, possibly causing flooding due to the polar ice caps melting.

Carbon dioxide (CO_2)

Water (H_2O)

Carbon Monoxide

Unlike carbon dioxide, a carbon monoxide molecule has only one oxygen atom attached to a carbon atom. Carbon monoxide is produced if there's not enough oxygen available when fuels burn.

Carbon monoxide is poisonous — if a dodgy boiler in your home starts giving out carbon monoxide, it can make you drowsy and headachey, and can even sometimes kill.

Carbon monoxide (CO)

Particulate Carbon

Often tiny particles of carbon are produced when fuels burn — this is called particulate carbon. If they escape into the atmosphere, which they often do, they just float around. Eventually they fall back to the ground and deposit themselves as the horrible black dust we call soot.

A lot of soot just falls onto buildings, making them look dirty, like this one.

Problems problems... there's always summat goin' wrong...

Burning fossil fuels produces lots of nasty polluting substances that float about in the air, making the world a dirty, poisonous place to live in. With this in mind, lots of energy companies are putting a lot of money into developing cleaner, renewable sources of energy, which will save the world. Hooray!

Pollution: Sulfur

Sulfur — it's dirty, nasty, pretty smelly, and you have to learn about it. No excuses.

Sulfur Pollution Comes from Impurities in Fuels

1) Many of our fuels are hydrocarbon-based, like petrol and natural gas. Some are just carbon-based, like coal. These fuels contain loads of impurities as they're extracted straight from the Earth's crust.

2) Many of these impurities are fairly harmless but some of them contain traces of the element sulfur.

3) When the fuel burns, the sulfur burns too. When sulfur atoms burn, they combine with the oxygen in the air to produce the pollutant sulfur dioxide.

4) So when power stations and vehicle engines burn up fossil fuels like coal and oil, small amounts of the pollutant sulfur dioxide are produced. This sulfur dioxide usually ends up in our atmosphere.

Look at all that gas — there's lots of sulfur dioxide in there, I bet.

Sulfur Pollution Causes Acid Rain

Sulfur dioxide has the formula SO_2. This tells you that a sulfur dioxide molecule comprises two oxygen atoms joined to one sulfur atom.

Sulfur dioxide (SO_2)

1) As with other pollutants, when sulfur dioxide gets into the atmosphere it will stay there until something gets rid of it.

2) The way sulfur dioxide usually leaves our atmosphere is in the form of acid rain.

3) When the sulfur dioxide emitted from vehicle engines and power stations reacts with the moisture in clouds, dilute sulfuric acid is formed.

4) Eventually this acid will fall as acid rain, which is bad news for buildings, plants, animals and humans.

5) Acid rain causes lakes to become acidic, killing plants and animals. It also kills trees and damages buildings and statues made from some kinds of stone like limestone.

Acid rain — well at least it's more exciting than carbon...

Sulfur, for those of you who might think otherwise, is spelt with an 'f'. So don't go writing 'sulphur' any more because we're spelling it like the Americans these days. Unfortunately it wasn't my decision, but I do as I'm told and I'm afraid you should too. So, from here on, it's sulfur to us both.

Pollution: Nitrogen

Now for a new type of pollution. One that, surprisingly, is made from the <u>nitrogen</u> in the <u>air</u> itself.

Nitrogen Pollution Involves Nitrogen from the Air

<u>Nitrogen pollution</u> comes from the nitrogen in the <u>air</u> itself, which gets messed up by burning <u>fossil fuels</u>:

1) Fossil fuels burn at such <u>high temperatures</u> that nearby <u>atoms</u> in the air <u>react</u> with each other.

2) <u>Nitrogen</u> in the air rarely reacts with anything. However, it does react with the <u>oxygen</u> in the air under extreme conditions, such as at the very high temperatures inside <u>engines</u> that burn <u>fossil fuels</u>.

3) When a car engine is running, <u>nitrogen</u> and <u>oxygen</u> <u>react</u> to produce small amounts of compounds known as <u>nitrogen oxides</u> — <u>nitrogen monoxide</u> and <u>nitrogen dioxide</u>.

4) Nitrogen oxides are <u>pollutants</u>, and are usually spewed straight out into the <u>atmosphere</u>.

Nitrogen Oxides Are Nitrogen Monoxide and Nitrogen Dioxide

1) <u>Nitrogen monoxide</u> has the formula NO — it is made of <u>one nitrogen</u> and <u>one oxygen</u> atom.

2) <u>Nitrogen dioxide</u> has the formula NO_2 — it is made of <u>two oxygen</u> atoms joined to <u>one nitrogen</u> atom.

3) <u>Nitrogen oxides</u> (NO and NO_2) can be jointly referred to as NO_x.

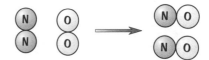

Nitrogen monoxide (NO)

Nitrogen dioxide (NO_2)

Here's exactly how nitrogen oxides are <u>formed</u>:

NITROGEN MONOXIDE

<u>Nitrogen monoxide</u> forms when <u>nitrogen</u> and <u>oxygen</u> in the air are exposed to a very <u>high temperature</u>. This happens when fuels are burnt in places like car <u>engines</u>.

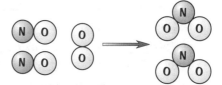

NITROGEN DIOXIDE

Once the nitrogen monoxide is in the air, it will go on to react with more <u>oxygen</u> in the air to produce <u>nitrogen dioxide</u>.

Nitrogen oxides are pollutants which are very similar to <u>sulfur dioxide</u>. When they are formed they usually end up in the atmosphere, which is where they stay until they <u>react</u> with <u>moisture</u> in the atmosphere. This produces a <u>dilute</u> <u>nitric acid</u> which eventually falls to the Earth as <u>acid rain</u>.

Aargh! Oh no! I'm melting!

Acid rain makes statues talk too.

I'll pollute you if you don't learn this...

Oh good — another type of <u>pollution</u> to learn about. Well, in my opinion, the only answer is to go back to the old days of farming a bit of land in a <u>self-sufficient</u> manner. No more <u>electricity</u>, no more industry, bliss. Although there'd be no more TVs, DVD players, X-ray machines, computers. Hmm, in that case...

Interpreting Pollution Data

Here's a page on the <u>reliability</u> of <u>scientific research</u> and why you shouldn't just trust what you read.

Claims About Air Pollution can be Difficult to Prove

Studies have found <u>air pollution</u> to cause lots of <u>health problems</u>. When such claims are made, there are three main reasons why we <u>shouldn't</u> immediately <u>trust</u> the research:

Data May be Disputed by Other Scientists

Imagine some scientists claimed that <u>air pollution</u> caused an increased number of <u>asthma attacks</u>:

1) Those scientists would have to provide <u>details</u> of the <u>experiments</u> they did and the <u>results</u> they got.

2) That's <u>not</u> enough though. To really <u>prove</u> it, <u>other</u> scientists would need to <u>repeat</u> the experiments and get the <u>same</u> results.

3) You need to know whether the scientists got their data using <u>accurate measurements</u> and reliable <u>equipment</u> and <u>methods</u>. Otherwise, you won't know whether the scientists just got <u>freak results</u> when they did their experiments.

4) You'll only know that you can <u>believe</u> the experiment's results if other scientists can <u>replicate</u> them.

Other Factors Might be Involved Too

Any outcome could also be <u>caused</u> by factors <u>other</u> than the one you're investigating. For example, air pollution isn't the only cause of asthma attacks.

1) It is thought that asthma attacks can be triggered by factors like high <u>pollen</u> levels, <u>infections</u> like colds and flu and even emotional <u>stress</u>.

Pollen — it has a lot to answer for.

2) Anything that <u>affects</u> these factors might also affect the <u>results</u> of any study of pollution levels and the number of asthma attacks.

3) Things that affect these factors should be <u>controlled</u> — for example, <u>pollen levels</u> should be checked before studies happen, and if they're <u>too high</u>, the study should be <u>delayed</u> until pollen levels are <u>lower</u>.

A Statistical Correlation Doesn't Always Mean a Causal Link

1) If there's a heat wave, the sales of cold drinks go up — it's fairly obvious. We say there is a <u>correlation</u> between temperature and drink sales. You can assume that the hot weather <u>caused</u> people to buy more cold drinks, so there's said to be a <u>causal link</u> between the two things.

2) The thing is... when the sales of cold drinks go up, the sales of swimwear increase too. There <u>is</u> a <u>correlation</u> between sales of cold drinks and sales of swimwear — as one goes up then so does the other. However, it's <u>not true</u> that one <u>caused</u> the other. The hot weather actually caused both.

3) So a correlation between two things <u>doesn't</u> necessarily mean that one <u>caused</u> the other.

4) Another fact to remember is that if there <u>is</u> a <u>causal link</u> between two things, it <u>doesn't</u> mean that one thing will <u>definitely</u> make the other thing happen.

5) For example, there's a <u>causal link</u> between revision and good grades, but doing lots of revision <u>doesn't</u> <u>guarantee</u> good grades, especially if you revise the wrong thing, forget to go to your exam etc.

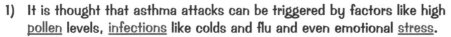
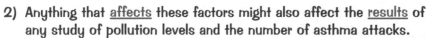

If you're studying <u>correlation</u>, it's important to get a <u>range of data</u>. If you want to prove that drink sales go up in summer, for instance, you need to make sure it is happening <u>everywhere</u>, not just in one shop.

There's a correlation between madness and chemistry knowledge...

Don't just believe what you read — ask questions like 'but how <u>reliable</u> was the experiment?', 'but could anything else have <u>caused</u> those results?' and 'but does that correlation show <u>causation</u>?'. Be <u>cynical</u> and doubt everything. This is how science works — scientists look for evidence for or against certain theories.

Reducing Pollution

Reducing pollution is very important. All this pollution is turning lovely Earth into a toxic rubbish dump.

Some Pollution can be Reduced Relatively Easily

Here are a few ways in which pollution can be reduced:

1) Sulfur can be taken out of natural gas and the fuel oil that power stations use. This means that no sulfur dioxide will be produced when it burns.

2) When coal is burnt in power stations, the sulfur dioxide and the particulates (carbon particles and ash) can be removed before they can get into the atmosphere.

3) Motor vehicles now have more efficient engines which burn less fuel and so create less pollution.

4) Low sulfur fuel for cars is now available, which means less sulfur dioxide is found in the exhaust gases.

5) Many cars are now fitted with catalytic converters. These convert harmful nitrogen monoxide into harmless nitrogen and oxygen. They also convert the very toxic gas carbon monoxide into the less harmful gas carbon dioxide.

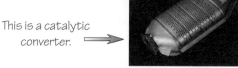

This is a catalytic converter.

ASTRID & HANNS-FRIEDER MICHLER / SCIENCE PHOTO LIBRARY

All of these pollution-reducing methods cost money to develop and produce, so they're only easy if you can afford to put them into action.

Bigger Changes May be Needed to Reduce Other Pollution

The only way to reduce CO_2 emissions is to reduce the amount of fossil fuels burnt. Changes like this need there to be a change in people's attitudes and behaviour, which takes time to happen. For example:

The less electricity we use, the less fossil fuel will need to be burnt in power stations, and the less pollution will be created. This sounds fairly simple to do but it would be very hard. We've all got used to consuming lots of electricity, and wouldn't enjoy giving up our TVs etc. Many people's jobs also depend on people using lots of electricity and electrical products.

We could also use less fossil fuel ourselves. If everyone used public transport instead of individual cars, for example, then less petrol would be burnt in cars. This would also reduce pollution overall. Again, this would not be very easy. It would be hard to persuade people to stop using their cars as personal cars are so convenient, often cost less than public transport and make people feel safer.

Changes in the Law Are Used to Control Pollution

Certain laws exist to make individuals and organisations responsible for the pollution they produce.

1) There's a legal limit on the amount of polluting emissions that cars can give out. A car's emissions are checked in the MOT test.

2) Any process that is likely to add pollutants to the atmosphere, including scientific research, must comply with laws and regulations that limit the amount of polluting chemicals that can be given out into the atmosphere.

Cars must pass an MOT test once a year to prove they're safe and not too polluting.

My brother is a major source of air pollution...

So... it doesn't sound like reducing pollution is going to be easy. We need to reduce the demand for electricity by not using so much of it, and then we won't need so many power stations. Start small by remembering to switch off lights, and don't leave stuff on standby — that's just wasting electricity.

Sustainable Development

Sustainable development is a hot topic at the moment — it's relevant to subjects like Geography too.

More People Means More Pressure on the Environment

1) The world's population is increasing at an amazing rate.

2) It has doubled in the last forty years and now totals 6.5 billion. It shows no sign of slowing down.

3) The more of us there are, the more food must be produced, the more fuel is burnt and the more land is used up. This all puts a lot of pressure on the environment.

Scientific Advances May Have Helped Cause the Problems...

Science-based technology has improved the quality of life for most of us, but is also unfortunately contributing to environmental problems. Computers are a good example of this:

1) Computers have made workplaces more efficient, and the internet has improved global communication, which is great for both individuals and businesses. Computers are still getting better all the time.

2) The trouble is that computers are full of poisonous substances. Computers don't last for ever and these poisonous substances cause a problem when it comes to computer disposal.

3) Many old computers are sent to poorer countries. There they are often dumped in landfills. This poisons the land for the people, animals and plants that live there.

Computers are great, as are many of the scientific advances that make our lives easier. However, the cost to the environment and ultimately to humans is massively important. Benefits need to be weighed against costs when deciding whether to use new technologies.

...But Other Advances Could Help us Live More Sustainably

Often science comes up with solutions to the problems it causes. In particular, science has helped us find ways of using our natural resources moderately so there is less chance of them running out for future generations. This is known as sustainable development. Here are some examples:

1) Scientific advances have allowed us to develop buildings that use less energy. For example, modern buildings have insulated windows and doors which mean less energy is used to heat them.

2) Using less energy means less fossil fuels are burnt in the building or at power stations and so less pollution reaches the atmosphere.

3) Buildings can also use renewable resources as energy sources, e.g. solar energy can be used to heat water and generate electricity. You can also buy wind turbines for your home to harness wind energy and generate electricity.

These days, there are laws and regulations governing scientific research. In many areas of science, scientists have to show that what they are developing will not go on to have an unacceptable impact on the environment. This particularly applies to pollutants being let into the atmosphere.

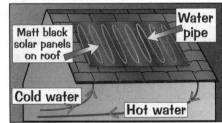

This is how solar panels could be used to heat the water in your house.

Try wind power — it can blow your mind...

It's kind of obvious that scientific development has led to environmental problems. I mean, back when there was little industry but lots of farming, fishing and stuff, there wasn't any pollution. But since then, every scientific advance has caused more problems — from pollution to cutting down rainforests.

Revision Summary for Module C1

Congratulations! You've made it through C1. You should now be an expert on fossil fuels, carbon, sulfur, air pollution and the general problems we're causing to the environment and our own health. You should also have picked up a little bit on atoms and what happens to them in chemical reactions. Anyway, maybe it's time you found out how much you do know. A good try at the questions below should give you some idea. Here we go...

1)   What three main gases is the atmosphere made of and in what proportions are they found?

2)   Name a couple of different hydrocarbons. What exactly makes them different?

3)   True or false — Coal is made of a mixture of carbon, hydrogen and nitrogen?

4)   When fuels burn, with what substance in the air do the hydrogen and carbon atoms combine?

5)   When hydrocarbons burn, the atoms involved rearrange themselves into carbon dioxide and what else?

6)   What do the numbers in symbol equations tell you?

7)   True or false — Atoms can disappear completely during certain chemical reactions?

8)   Are the properties of reactants and products always the same or can they be different?

9)   Name one result of pollution which causes direct harm to humans, and one which causes indirect harm.

10) Is there any way of removing carbon dioxide from the atmosphere?

11) What atoms make up carbon monoxide? When is carbon monoxide produced?

12) What are particles of carbon otherwise known as and what kind of pollution do they cause?

13) Describe briefly how the pollutant sulfur dioxide is produced.

14) True or false — Sulfur dioxide leaves the atmosphere in the form of acid rain?

15) What effects does acid rain have on the environment?

16) In nitrogen pollution, where exactly do the nitrogen atoms come from?

17) Give the formulas of nitrogen monoxide and nitrogen dioxide.

18) What effect do nitrogen oxides have on the environment?

19)* Why should you question the results of an experiment if the experiment was only done once?

20)*If a rise in asthma attacks is seen, what could have caused it?

21) True or false — If air pollution increases and so does cancer, that means air pollution causes cancer?

22) What do catalytic converters do?

23) Name two things that everyone should be doing in order to reduce carbon dioxide pollution.

24) How do MOT tests help combat air pollution?

25) Why is it a problem that the human population is rapidly increasing?

26) Give an example of a scientific advancement that contributes to environmental problems.

27) What is sustainable development?

28) Give an example of a renewable resource that could be used to provide energy for our homes.

* Answers on page 104.

The Changing Earth

There are some really <u>dull</u> things in our Solar System. For example, <u>asteroids</u> don't do much except go round and round the Sun. The <u>Earth</u>, however, is <u>different</u>...

The Earth is an Active Planet

1) It's kind of tempting to think that the Earth is a <u>steady</u>, <u>unchanging</u> place that'll always look pretty much as it does now.

2) But no... in a few tens of millions of years, Earth's going to look a <u>lot</u> different.

3) <u>Mountains</u> that are <u>enormous</u> today won't be nearly so grand. And the map of the world will be very different — whole <u>continents</u> will have <u>moved</u>. Weird.

4) This isn't anything new — Earth's been changing for <u>thousands of millions</u> of years.

Rocks Provide a Record of Changes in the Earth

Rocks <u>change</u> over the years, and provide clues about the <u>history</u> of the <u>Earth</u>.

1) Look at the <u>Grand Canyon</u>, for example. Over time, the Colorado River has <u>eroded</u> (worn away) the rock, leaving an impressive slash through the middle of <u>Arizona</u>.

2) Erosion goes on <u>everywhere</u>. We see it happening, for example, when <u>cliffs</u> are worn away by the <u>sea</u>. But <u>other</u> processes must be happening as well. If not, all the mountains would have been <u>worn down</u> by now... Earth would be <u>perfectly smooth</u>.

3) So something must be making <u>new</u> rock. And <u>evidence</u> is pretty easy to find — e.g. when <u>lava</u> from <u>volcanoes</u> sets, it forms brand new rock.

4) <u>Fossils</u> also provide evidence that rock is constantly forming. The animals and plants couldn't have <u>dug themselves</u> into the <u>middle</u> of rocks — the <u>rocks</u> must have <u>built up</u> around them.

Fossils are traces of animals and plants from long ago. They're most commonly found in rocks.

Rocks are Being Constantly Recycled

In fact, evidence suggests rocks are <u>constantly</u> changing and being <u>recycled</u> — in the 'rock cycle'.

1) Particles <u>eroded</u> from existing rock (e.g. by water flowing over them) get washed into the <u>sea</u> and <u>settle</u> as <u>sediment</u>. Over time, these sediments get <u>crushed</u> together to form <u>sedimentary rocks</u>.

2) These can get <u>pushed</u> to the surface, or they can <u>descend</u> into the <u>heat</u> and <u>pressure</u> inside the Earth. If they descend, the <u>structure</u> of the rock can change completely as it gets <u>heated</u> and <u>crushed</u>. Sometimes the rock actually <u>melts</u> (but will <u>solidify</u> into new rock if it <u>cools</u>, e.g. near Earth's surface).

DR MORLEY READ /
SCIENCE PHOTO LIBRARY

3) When any of these rocks are pushed up to reach the <u>surface</u>, the cycle starts again — they gradually get <u>worn down</u> and <u>carried off</u> to the sea again... and so on.

4) The rock cycle needs some very powerful <u>forces</u> to <u>push</u> rock up or down as described — but there's very good evidence that this is what happens. For example, some rock formations show rock that's been squeezed so hard it's just <u>folded</u>.

Scientists Can Use Radioactivity to Tell How Old Rocks Are

1) By looking at the proportions of <u>radioactive</u> potassium-40, and the element it <u>decays</u> into, in certain rocks, scientists can get a good idea of when they were <u>formed</u>. (It's tricky, but it can be done.)

2) The <u>oldest</u> rocks found so far that were made on Earth are about 4 billion (4 000 000 000) years or so old. So the Earth must have been around for <u>at least</u> that long. Wowzers.

If you want to see the Rocky Mountains, don't leave it too long...

<u>Erosion</u> will eventually wear down the <u>Rockies</u> — in a few million years they <u>won't be there</u>. Shame. There's more about what causes the <u>forces</u> responsible for all the pushing up and down of rock on page 30. And there's more evidence about <u>how</u> and <u>why</u> Earth changes on p.29. It's all exciting stuff.

Observations and Explanations

Observations and explanations aren't the same. Anyone can observe something, but explaining it is trickier. Take the Earth for instance — for years, scientists knew there were things about it they didn't understand.

Observations About the Earth Hadn't Been Explained

1) For years, fossils of very similar plants and animals had been found on opposite sides of the Atlantic Ocean. Most people thought this was because the continents had been linked by 'land bridges', which had sunk or been covered by water as the Earth cooled. But not everyone was convinced, even back then.

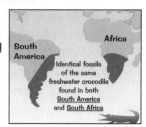

Identical fossils of the same freshwater crocodile found in both South America and South Africa

2) Other things about the Earth also puzzled people — like why the coastlines of Africa and South America matched so well. And why fossils from sea creatures had been found high in the Alps.

Explaining These Observations Needed a Leap of Imagination

What was needed was a scientist with a bit of insight... a smidgeon of creativity... a touch of genius...

1) Alfred Wegener hypothesised that Africa and South America had previously been one continent which had then split. He started to look for more evidence to back up his hypothesis. He found it...

2) E.g. there were matching layers in the rocks on different continents, and similar earthworms living in both South America and South Africa.

3) Wegener published his theory of "continental drift" saying that about 300 million years ago, there had been just one 'supercontinent' — called Pangaea. According to Wegener, Pangaea broke into smaller chunks which moved apart... and these chunks (our modern-day continents) were still slowly 'drifting' apart.

The Theory Wasn't Accepted at First — for a Variety of Reasons

1) Wegener's theory explained things that couldn't be explained by the 'land bridge' theory (e.g. the formation of mountains — which Wegener said happened as continents smashed into each other). But it was a big change, and the reaction from other scientists was hostile.

2) The main problem was that Wegener's explanation of how the 'drifting' happened wasn't convincing (and the movement wasn't detectable). Wegener claimed the continents' movement could be caused by tidal forces and the Earth's rotation — but other geologists showed that this was impossible.

3) Also, it probably didn't help that Wegener wasn't a 'proper' geologist — he was a meteorologist.

Eventually, the Evidence Became Overwhelming

1) In the 1950s, scientists investigated the Mid-Atlantic ridge, which runs the whole length of the Atlantic.

2) They found evidence that magma (molten rock) rises up through the sea floor, solidifies and forms underwater mountains that are roughly symmetrical either side of the ridge. The evidence suggested that the sea floor was spreading — at about 10 cm per year.

3) Even better evidence that the continents are moving apart came from the magnetic orientation of the rocks. As the liquid magma erupts out of the gap, iron particles in the rocks tend to align themselves with the Earth's magnetic field — and as it cools they set in position. Now then... every half million years or so the Earth's magnetic field swaps direction — and the rock on either side of the ridge has bands of alternate magnetic polarity, symmetrical about the ridge.

4) This was convincing evidence that new sea floor was being created... and continents were moving apart.

I told you so — but no one ever believes me...

Wegener wasn't right about everything, but his main idea was correct. Nowadays, we know that it's not just the continents that move, but whole tectonic plates (including oceans) — see the next page.

The Structure of the Earth

We can tell a lot about what goes on deep inside the Earth by looking at what happens on the surface.

The Earth Has a Crust, Mantle and Core

The Earth is almost spherical and it has a layered structure, a bit like a scotch egg. Or a peach.

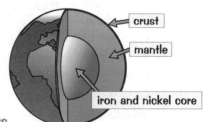

1) The bit we live on, the crust, is very thin (about 20 km). There are two types of crust — continental crust (forming the land), and oceanic crust (under oceans).

2) Below that is the mantle. The mantle has all the properties of a solid, except that it can flow very slowly.

3) Within the mantle, radioactive decay takes place. This produces a lot of heat, which causes the mantle to flow in convection currents.

4) At the centre of the Earth is the core, which we think is made of mainly iron and nickel.

The Earth's Surface is Made Up of Tectonic Plates

1) The crust and the upper part of the mantle are cracked into a number of large pieces called tectonic plates. These plates are a bit like big rafts that 'float' on the mantle.

2) The plates don't stay in one place though. That's because the convection currents in the mantle cause the plates to drift.

3) The map shows the edges of the plates as they are now, and the directions they're moving in (red arrows).

4) Most of the plates are moving at speeds of a few cm per year relative to each other.

5) Occasionally, the plates move very suddenly, causing an earthquake. Volcanoes often form at the boundaries between two tectonic plates too.

6) And as plates crash into each other, mountains are formed. For example, the Himalayas are where India is crashing into the Eurasian plate — the Himalayas are still growing by a centimetre or two per year as India keeps moving northwards. Similar collisions created the Alps and the Pyrenees.

7) These processes also contribute to the rock cycle — pushing rock down, or up to Earth's surface. Where the plates collide, one often gets pushed underneath the other.

Scientists Try to Predict Earthquakes and Volcanic Eruptions

1) Tectonic plates can stay put for a while and then suddenly lurch forwards without warning to cause an earthquake. Volcanoes can be very unpredictable too.

2) Scientists are trying to find out if there are any clues that an earthquake or volcanic eruption might happen soon — things like strain in underground rocks or magma movement under a volcano.

3) But it's tricky. Most likely, scientists will only be able to say that an earthquake or volcanic eruption's more likely — but not that it's certain.

4) However, knowing even just a little about whether an earthquake or eruption is likely could save lives. If disaster's likely to strike soon (or even soonish), the authorities can warn residents and evacuate the area.

Learn about plate tectonics — but don't get carried away...

It's important to remember that earthquakes and volcanoes are unpredictable, even with the best equipment in the world. However, even a little information about the likelihood of an eruption or earthquake would be potentially useful. Learn all the information — you're going to need it.

The Solar System

What a fantastic place Earth is. But the rest of our Solar System is pretty cool too.

Planets Reflect Sunlight and Orbit the Sun in Ellipses

Our solar system consists of a star (the Sun) and lots of stuff orbiting it in slightly elongated circles.

- Closest to the Sun are the inner planets — Mercury, Venus, Earth and Mars.
- Then the asteroid belt — see below.
- Then the outer planets, much further away — Jupiter, Saturn, Uranus, Neptune, Pluto.
- There's also various other things — comets, dust, meteors and so on... all in orbit around the Sun. These also count as part of our Solar System.

Stars and Planets are Very Different

1) You can see some planets with the naked eye. They look like stars, but they're totally different.
2) Stars are huge (the Sun's diameter is over 100 times bigger than the Earth's), very hot and very far away. They give out lots of light — which is why you can see them even though they're far away.
3) Planets are smaller and they just reflect sunlight falling on them. The planets in the Solar System are also much much closer to us than any star (except the Sun).
4) Planets often have moons orbiting them. Jupiter has at least 63 of 'em. We've just got one.

The Solar System is About 5 Billion Years Old — We Think

1) The Solar System was formed from a big cloud of dust.
2) For some reason (maybe a nearby star exploding), this dust cloud started to get squeezed slightly.
3) Once the particles had moved a bit closer to each other, gravity took over. It pulled things closer and closer together until the whole cloud started to collapse in on itself.
4) At the centre of the collapse, particles came together to form a protostar, which went on to become our Sun (see page 35). Elsewhere, dust started to clump together — and these clumps became planets. (So the Sun and the planets are similar ages.)
5) The oldest rocks on Earth actually came from meteorites (rocks from space that crashed into Earth — we think they were formed not long after the birth of the Solar System). These are about 4.6 billion years old — so we know the Solar System is at least that old.

Asteroids and Comets are Smaller Than Most Planets

1) Asteroids and comets are made of stuff left over from the formation of the Solar System.
2) The rocks between Mars and Jupiter didn't form a planet, but stayed as smallish lumps of rubble and rock — these are asteroids.

Comet

3) Comets are balls of rock, dust and ice which orbit the Sun in very elongated ellipses, often in different planes from the planets. The Sun is near one end of the orbit.
4) As a comet approaches the Sun, its ice melts, leaving a bright tail of gas and debris which can be millions of kilometres long. This is what we see from Earth.

Asteroids... my dad had those — very nasty...

So one minute there was a big cloud of dust... the next there were planets, a star, asteroids, comets and all sorts. Okay... it actually took hundreds of millions of years, but it's still pretty impressive.

Danger from Space

If anything from space hit the Earth, it <u>could</u> be unpleasant. The <u>atmosphere</u> provides some protection against <u>smaller</u> things, but if something <u>bigger</u> hit, the consequences could be <u>bad</u>.

Earth is Sometimes Hit by Rocks and Dust

1) There's a lot of stuff floating about in space — ranging in size from <u>specks of dust</u> to huge <u>asteroids</u>.

2) Quite often, small particles of dust or small rocks enter the Earth's <u>atmosphere</u>. On their way through the atmosphere they usually <u>burn up</u> — and we see them as '<u>shooting stars</u>'.

3) Sometimes, not all of the object burns up and part of it crashes into the <u>Earth's surface</u>. This only happens <u>rarely</u>, but when large things do hit us, they can cause <u>havoc</u>...

   • They can cause huge <u>tsunamis</u> if they land in the ocean. On land they can start <u>fires</u>, and throw loads of <u>hot rocks</u> and <u>dust</u> into the air.

   • The <u>dust</u> and <u>smoke</u> from a large impact can <u>block out</u> the <u>sunlight</u> for many months, causing <u>climate change</u> — which in turn can cause <u>species</u> to become <u>extinct</u>.

   • They also make big <u>holes</u> in the ground (<u>craters</u>, if we're being technical).

©iStockphoto.com/Stephan Hoerold

   The picture shows an <u>impact crater</u> in Arizona. The theory that this was the result of a <u>collision</u> with an object from space took a while to be <u>accepted</u> (as is often the case with new claims). But <u>evidence</u> eventually emerged to convince the doubters.

4) We can tell that asteroids have collided with Earth in the past. There are the <u>big craters</u>, but also:

   • layers of <u>unusual elements</u> in rocks — these must have been 'imported' by an asteroid,

   • sudden changes in <u>fossil numbers</u> between adjacent layers of rock, as species suffer extinction.

Impact was about here...

About 65 million years ago an asteroid about <u>10 km across</u> struck the <u>Yucatán peninsula</u> in Mexico. The dust it kicked up caused global temperatures to plummet, and over half the species on Earth subsequently died out (including maybe the last of the <u>dinosaurs</u>).

A Really Big Impact is Very Unlikely in Your Lifetime

1) Astronomers use <u>powerful telescopes</u> to search for and monitor <u>asteroids</u> or <u>comets</u> which <u>might</u> be on a <u>collision course</u> with Earth. Then they can calculate an object's <u>likely trajectory</u> (the path it's probably going to take) and find out if it's <u>actually</u> anything to worry about.

2) Scientists can also get an idea about the likelihood of something hitting Earth by looking at the <u>Moon</u>. The Moon has <u>no atmosphere</u> for objects to burn up in, and so impact craters are much <u>more common</u> on the Moon than on Earth. Also, the Moon's craters don't get <u>eroded</u> by water or wind, or disturbed in other ways, e.g. by volcanoes.

3) In the last <u>600 million years</u>, Earth has probably been hit by <u>60 or so</u> objects more than 5 km across. And an impact like the one in the Yucatán peninsula happens about only <u>once</u> every <u>300 million years</u>.

4) So the odds of a really big impact with Earth within the next century are <u>tiny</u>. And if scientists did find something worrying heading for us, we'd most likely have <u>decades</u> (or maybe <u>centuries</u>) of <u>warning</u>.

...Eeek...?

5) <u>Smaller</u> impacts are <u>more frequent</u>. An object of the size that made the Arizona crater hits every <u>160 years</u> or so. Something that size <u>wouldn't</u> cause worldwide devastation, though (but it would trash the <u>immediate surroundings</u>).

Don't go to the Moon for a night out — there's no atmosphere...

When a big object's discovered that <u>might</u> be heading in Earth's direction, the newspaper headlines tend to be fairly <u>dramatic</u>. But you need to keep this kind of thing in some kind of perspective... For example, an object was found a few years ago that had a <u>1 in 40</u> chance of hitting Earth. But remember, the odds were <u>39 in 40</u> (i.e. 97.5%) that it <u>wouldn't</u> hit, which is <u>far more likely</u> (though less newsworthy).

Beyond the Solar System

There's all sorts of exciting stuff out there. The whole Solar System is just part of one <u>galaxy</u>. And there are <u>billions upon billions</u> of galaxies. Yup, the <u>Universe</u> is big — huge in fact...

We're in the Milky Way Galaxy

1) Our <u>Sun</u> is just one of <u>many billions</u> of <u>stars</u> which form the <u>Milky Way galaxy</u>. The Sun is about halfway along one of the <u>spiral arms</u> of the Milky Way.

2) The <u>distance</u> between neighbouring stars in a galaxy is usually <u>millions of times greater</u> than the distance between <u>planets</u> in the Solar System.

3) And the diameter of the Milky Way is about 600 billion times the diameter of the Sun. Yup... it's pretty big.

4) The <u>force</u> which keeps the stars together in a galaxy is <u>gravity</u>. And like most things in the Universe, galaxies <u>rotate</u> — a bit like Catherine wheels.

The Whole Universe Has More Than a Billion Galaxies

1) Galaxies themselves are often <u>millions of times</u> further apart than the stars are within a galaxy.

2) So even the slowest among you will have worked out that the Universe is <u>mostly empty space</u> and is <u>really really BIG</u>.

3) The Universe is also really really <u>old</u> — about <u>14 billion</u> years old, according to scientists' latest theories (see p.36).

Distances in Space Can Be Measured Using Light Years

1) Once you get outside our Solar System, the distances between stars and between galaxies are <u>so enormous</u> that kilometres seem too <u>pathetically small</u> for measuring them.

2) For example, the <u>closest</u> star to us (after the Sun) is about 40 000 000 000 000 kilometres away (give or take a few hundred billion kilometres). Numbers like that soon get out of hand.

3) So we use <u>light years</u> instead. A <u>light year</u> is the <u>distance</u> that <u>light travels</u> through a vacuum (like space) in one <u>year</u>. Simple as that.

4) If you work it out, 1 light year is equal to about 9 460 000 000 000 kilometres. Which means the closest star after the Sun is about <u>4.2 light years</u> away from us.

5) Just remember — a light year is a measure of <u>DISTANCE</u> (<u>not</u> time).

There Might be Other Life in the Universe

1) It's possible that <u>life</u> exists <u>elsewhere</u> in the Universe. After all, when you consider the how <u>huge</u> the Universe is, why should our planet be the <u>only</u> place with suitable conditions...

2) Scientists believe conditions <u>necessary</u> for life (e.g. water, nutrients...) are most likely to be found on other <u>planets</u>, or on <u>moons</u>. So they started a search for planets outside the Solar System.

3) So far, about 185 planets have been discovered <u>orbiting</u> nearby <u>stars</u>. It's <u>very</u> likely there are a <u>lot</u> more, given how many stars there are. <u>Maybe</u> some of these planets or their moons could be <u>inhabited</u>. But so far it's just a <u>theory</u> — we <u>haven't</u> found other life yet.

4) However, some scientists believe the Sun and the Earth are actually <u>pretty special</u> e.g. the Sun's <u>position</u> in the Milky Way keeps us away from too much <u>radiation</u>, and the Earth's unusual <u>tectonic activity</u> is a great way to recycle the <u>carbon</u> needed for life. These features are <u>very helpful</u> but <u>very unlikely</u>, and so suitable conditions for life <u>may</u> not be as common as you'd think.

Spiral arms — would you still need elbows...

Until we actually discover life elsewhere, the debate about whether it exists or not is likely to continue. Proving life <u>does</u> exist is relatively 'easy' — you find life and the argument's over. But it's impossible to prove beyond doubt that life <u>doesn't</u> exist elsewhere — after all, there are plenty of places it <u>could</u> be.

Looking into Space

We can't <u>travel to</u> stars to study them — it'd take 'a while' (thousands of years, at the very least). All we can realistically do is measure the <u>radiation</u> coming <u>from</u> them.

Radiation Can Tell Us a Lot About Stars and Galaxies

1) We can tell a lot about a star by studying the <u>electromagnetic radiation</u> (e.g. light, X-rays, radio waves — see p.58) it emits. For example, the <u>colour</u> that a star appears is actually a pretty good guide to its <u>temperature</u>.

Big dish telescopes like these are for detecting radio waves.

2) To work out <u>how far away</u> a star is, you can use various methods.

3) For 'nearby' stars, you can use <u>parallax</u>. Astronomers take <u>pictures</u> of the sky 6 months apart (when Earth is at <u>opposite sides</u> of its orbit).

<u>Parallax</u> is when something <u>appears to move</u> when you look at it from <u>different places</u> (e.g. hold your finger at arm's length and look at it first through your left eye, then your right — it seems to move against the background).

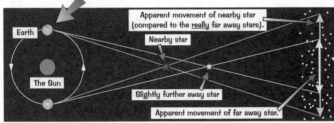

Earth
Apparent movement of nearby star (compared to the really far away stars).
Nearby star
The Sun
Slightly further away star
Apparent movement of far away star.

4) The <u>apparent movement</u> of a star between the two photos lets you work out <u>how far away</u> it is. Stars <u>further away</u> appear to move less (the <u>really</u> distant stars don't appear to move at all — the movement is too small to detect).

5) Another way to get an idea of the distance to a star is to measure its <u>brightness</u>. Unfortunately, a star that <u>looks</u> very bright to us here on Earth could be either:
   a) quite <u>close</u> to Earth but <u>not</u> actually that <u>bright</u>, or b) a <u>long way away</u> and <u>very bright indeed</u>. However, astronomers know <u>how much radiation</u> certain types of star <u>actually</u> emit, and so by examining how bright they look <u>from Earth</u>, they can tell <u>how far away</u> that star must be.

The Atmosphere and Light Pollution Cause Some Problems

1) If you're trying to detect <u>light</u>, Earth's <u>atmosphere</u> can be a bit of a pain — it <u>absorbs</u> quite a bit of the light coming from space <u>before</u> it can reach us.

2) And <u>light pollution</u> (light thrown upwards from streetlamps, etc.) makes it <u>hard</u> to see <u>dim</u> objects.

3) That's why scientists put the <u>Hubble Space Telescope</u> in <u>space</u> — where you don't get these problems.

We See Stars and Galaxies as They Were in the Past

1) <u>Electromagnetic radiation</u> (including light) travels pretty <u>fast</u> — in a vacuum it goes at about <u>300 000 km per second</u>. (Something travelling at that speed would go right around the Earth in about 0.13 seconds.)

2) Since the <u>Sun</u> is about 150 million km away from Earth, the radiation from the Sun that <u>reaches us</u> must have left about <u>8 minutes</u> before we actually see it.

3) That means that when we look at the Sun, we see it as it was <u>about 8 minutes ago</u>. So if it suddenly exploded (but, fingers crossed, it won't for a while), we wouldn't know <u>anything</u> about it for <u>about 8 minutes</u>.

4) Since the nearest star to us after the Sun is about <u>4.2 light years</u> away, light from it takes <u>4.2 years</u> to reach us. This means we see it as it was <u>4.2 years ago</u>.

5) When we look at other stars, this effect is even more extreme. For example, we see the <u>North Star</u> as it was during the time of <u>William Shakespeare</u> (it's about 431 light years away).

Constant stars, in them I read such art... (From Shakespeare's Julius Caesar.)

A bit of culture there. Now then... measuring the distance to a star is <u>very hard</u> (especially ones that are really far away) — scientists have to make certain <u>assumptions</u> about the <u>star</u> and about the <u>space</u> between it and Earth. What this means is that there's a <u>degree of uncertainty</u> in those measurements. So if someone says they know to the <u>nearest kilometre</u> how far away a star in a distant galaxy is, they're lying.

The Life Cycle of Stars

Stars go through many traumatic stages in their lives — you don't need to learn the details, but you do need to know that all stars go through a life cycle something like this...

Clouds of Dust and Gas

1) Stars initially form from clouds of DUST AND GAS.

Protostar

2) Gravity makes the gas and dust spiral together to form a hot ball called a protostar.

Stable Star

3) When the temperature gets high enough, a process called fusion starts — hydrogen nuclei join together to make helium. This gives out massive amounts of heat and light... a star is born. It immediately enters a long stable period that lasts several billion years. (The Sun is in the middle of this stable period — or to put it another way, the Earth has already had half its innings before the Sun engulfs it!)

Red Giant

4) Eventually the star runs out of hydrogen and swells into a RED GIANT.

Small stars ➡ White Dwarf

Big stars

5) A small-to-medium-sized star like the Sun then throws off its outer layers to leave behind a hot, dense core — a WHITE DWARF, which cools down and eventually disappears (awww...).

Neutron Star... ➡ ...or Black Hole

Supernova

6) Big stars, however, eventually explode in a SUPERNOVA.

7) The exploding supernova leaves behind a very dense core called a NEUTRON STAR. If the star is big enough this will become a BLACK HOLE.

I'm sure there must be easier ways to become a star...

Elements heavier than helium are only made in the final stages of a big star, just before the supernova. So the presence of heavy elements in our Solar System would suggest that our beautiful, wonderful world, with its warm sunsets and fresh morning dews, is formed from the snotty remains of a grisly old star's dying sneeze.

The Life of the Universe

They expect you to know all about the history of the Earth, the Solar System, stars... and the <u>Universe</u>. Sheesh... they don't give these GCSEs away easily, do they.

The <u>Universe</u> Seems to be <u>Expanding</u>

1) The Universe is pretty big already. But it looks like it's getting <u>even bigger</u> all the time.
2) All its <u>galaxies</u> seem to be moving away from each other.
3) Also, it would appear that the <u>more distant</u> galaxies are <u>moving away faster</u> than nearer ones. (This is Hubble's Law — named after Edwin Hubble, a famous astronomer.)
4) The inescapable <u>conclusion</u> appears to be that the whole Universe is <u>expanding</u>.

The Evidence Suggests the Universe <u>Started</u> <u>with a Bang</u>

All the galaxies are moving away from each other at great speed... suggesting something must have <u>got them going</u> in the first place. That 'something' was probably a <u>big explosion</u> — the <u>Big Bang</u>.

1) The Big Bang theory says that all the matter in the Universe initially occupied <u>a very small space</u> (<u>all</u> the matter in <u>all</u> the galaxies squashed into a space <u>much much smaller</u> than a pin-head — <u>wowzers</u>). Then it '<u>exploded</u>' — the space started expanding, and the <u>expansion</u> is still going on.
2) Using the Big Bang theory, we can estimate the <u>age</u> of the Universe. From the current <u>rate of expansion</u>, we think the Universe is about <u>14 billion years</u> old.
3) But estimating the age of the Universe is <u>very difficult</u> because it's hard to tell how much the expansion has <u>slowed down</u> since the Big Bang.

We <u>Don't Know How (or If)</u> the Universe Will End...

1) The Universe's ultimate fate depends on <u>how fast</u> it's expanding and the <u>total mass</u> there is in it.
2) We can measure the <u>expansion</u> quite easily (relatively speaking). But finding out <u>how much mass</u> there is in the Universe is a bit trickier.
3) Most of the mass appears to be <u>invisible</u> — it <u>doesn't glow</u> like a star. Astronomers can only detect this <u>dark matter</u> by the way it <u>affects the movement</u> of the things we <u>can</u> see.
4) The <u>amount</u> of dark matter in the Universe (as well as what it actually <u>is</u>) is one of the great unanswered questions in science. And it matters (no pun intended), because it's the amount of mass in the Universe that will dictate what happens to the Universe in the future.
5) This is because all the mass <u>everywhere</u> is attracted together by gravity. The more mass there is, the greater this pull, and the greater the slowing down of the Universe's <u>expansion</u>.

- If there's <u>enough mass</u> compared to <u>how fast</u> the galaxies are currently moving, the Universe will eventually <u>stop expanding</u> — and then <u>begin contracting</u>. This would end in a <u>Big Crunch</u>.
- If there's <u>not enough mass</u> in the Universe to stop the expansion, it could <u>expand forever</u>, with the Universe becoming <u>more and more spread out</u> into eternity.

In the beginning, there was... well, it's so hard to tell...

In fact (and this is a bit weird, I admit), according to recent observations, the Universe seems to be expanding <u>faster and faster</u>, <u>not</u> slowing down at all. What's going on there? We have no idea. But it shows how new evidence (if <u>confirmed</u> by other observations) makes scientists rethink their theories.

The Scientific Community

Who decides which scientific theories are <u>sound</u>, and which are <u>nonsense</u>... The '<u>scientific community</u>', that's who. Let me explain, using the very simple (hmmm...) example of the beginning of the Universe...

Observations *About the Universe Needed an Explanation*

1) For years, many scientists (including Einstein) had believed that the Universe was <u>static</u> and <u>unchanging</u> (kind of how people thought of the Earth before Wegener).

2) So the <u>observations</u> that distant galaxies appear to be moving <u>away</u> from us were pretty important. This meant the Universe <u>couldn't</u> be unchanging — so a <u>new</u> theory was needed.

Different Scientists *Came Up With Different Explanations*

1) Scientists <u>accepted</u> that the Universe was <u>expanding</u> (<u>similar results</u> had been found before), and that an <u>explanation</u> was needed — but <u>different people</u> came up with <u>different explanations</u>.

2) One theory was the <u>Big Bang</u> theory — the Universe was originally squashed into a tiny space, which then exploded... and the expansion is still going on.

3) Another theory was the <u>Steady State</u> theory.
You don't need to learn the details, but basically, this said that the Universe had always existed (and would always exist) pretty much as it is now — there was no huge explosion. It agreed that the Universe <u>was</u> expanding, but said that it <u>always had been</u>. However, matter was being <u>created</u> in the gaps, so it never actually <u>looked</u> any different.

Scientists Were *Divided* — *Until* New Evidence *Was Found*

1) Now then... the scientific process depends on '<u>peer review</u>'. This means that scientific theories are <u>judged</u> by the <u>scientific community</u> (all the world's scientists). If you can <u>convince</u> the scientific community, then your theory will be <u>accepted</u> (for the time being at least).

2) Traditionally, new findings and theories are announced in <u>peer-reviewed</u> <u>journals</u>, or at <u>scientific conferences</u>.

> A <u>peer-reviewed</u> journal is one where <u>other scientists</u> check results and theories <u>before</u> they're published. They check that people have been '<u>scientific</u>' about what they're saying — e.g. that experiments and claims aren't <u>biased</u>. But this doesn't mean that the findings are <u>correct</u>, just that they're not wrong in an <u>obvious</u> kind of way.

3) Anyway... in 1959, opinion in the scientific community on the nature of the Universe was <u>divided</u>.
In a poll of astronomers, 11 were for the Big Bang, 8 for the Steady State, and 14 weren't sure what to believe. The way the scientific community jumped would depend on what other <u>evidence</u> came to light.

4) To <u>test</u> the Big Bang theory, scientists <u>predicted</u> that there should be some 'leftover radiation' from the initial explosion, and that it should be at a particular temperature. When they <u>found</u> it some years later, it was <u>strong evidence</u> that the Big Bang was the more likely explanation of the two.

5) Today <u>nearly all</u> astronomers agree there <u>was</u> a Big Bang. However, there are <u>some</u> who still believe in the Steady State theory. Some of these say the <u>evidence</u> just points that way. Others maybe <u>don't</u> <u>want to change their mind</u> — that would mean admitting they were <u>wrong</u> in the first place.

Scientists Will *Stick* with the *Big Bang Theory...* *(Unless there's a better idea)*

1) The Big Bang theory <u>isn't perfect</u>. As it stands, it's <u>not</u> the whole explanation of the Universe — there are observations that the theory can't yet explain. But it's most likely the Big Bang theory will be <u>adapted</u> in some way to account for these rather than just <u>dumped</u> — it explains so much so well that scientists will need a lot of persuading to drop it altogether.

2) However, if someone comes up with a revolutionary <u>new</u> idea that <u>explains the observations</u> in a much more convincing way, then who knows...

Time and space — it's funny old stuff isn't it...

<u>Proving</u> a scientific theory is impossible. If enough evidence points a certain way, then a theory can look pretty <u>convincing</u>. But that doesn't <u>prove</u> it's a <u>fact</u> — <u>new evidence</u> may change people's minds.

Revision Summary for Module P1

The only way you can tell if you've learned this module is to test yourself. Try these questions, and if there's something you don't know, go back and learn it. Even if it is all that tricky business about the origins of the Universe. And don't miss any questions out — you don't get a choice about what comes up on the exam so you need to be sure that you've learnt it all.

1) Describe one piece of evidence that shows that rocks are constantly being:
   a) worn down,   b) made.

2) Give a brief description of the 'rock cycle'.

3) How can scientists tell how old some rocks are?
   What does this tell us about when the Earth was formed?

4) Describe two observations about the Earth that weren't properly explained by the 'land bridge' theory.

5) How did Alfred Wegener's theory account for these observations?

6) Suggest why the initial reaction to Wegener's theory was hostile.

7) What evidence led scientists to accept most of Wegener's theory about the movement of continents?

8) Draw a labelled diagram showing the layered structure of the Earth.

9) What are tectonic plates? Why do they move? What can these movements cause?

10)* Why is it so tricky to predict earthquakes accurately?

11) What's the difference between a planet and a star? And what are asteroids and comets?

12) How do scientists think the Solar System was originally formed?

13) How can we tell that objects from space have hit the Earth?
    How do scientists work out if another impact is likely soon?

14) What's the Milky Way? What holds the Milky Way together?

15) What's a light year?

16) What can scientists currently say about life elsewhere in the Universe? Explain your answer.

17) Describe two ways in which scientists can tell how far away from Earth a star is.

18) Why do we see stars as they were in the past?

19) What happens inside a star to make it so hot?

20) Describe the steps that lead to the formation of a main sequence star (like our Sun).

21) Describe the 'Big Bang' theory for the origin of the Universe. What evidence is there for this theory?

22) How are 'black holes' formed from stars? Why are they called 'black'?
    Why will our Sun never form a black hole?

23)* Who judges whether to accept or reject a new scientific theory? What is 'peer-review'?

* Answers on page 104.

Microorganisms and Disease

If you have hypochondriac tendencies then you're going to love this section — it's all about diseases, mainly infectious diseases and heart disease, and the different ways to prevent them.

Microorganisms Cause Many Diseases

1) Lots of microorganisms cause disease. Microorganisms that cause disease are called pathogens.

2) They include some bacteria, protozoa (single-celled creatures), fungi and viruses.

3) All pathogens are parasites — they live off their host and give nothing in return.

4) Most microorganisms reproduce fastest in warm, damp places. This means that they tend to reproduce very quickly inside host organisms.

5) Once pathogens get inside their host and start reproducing they cause an infection.

6) Some kinds of pathogen take longer to cause an infection than others.

Lovely bacteria — all floaty woaty.

Symptoms Can Be Caused by Cell Damage or by Toxins

1) The effects that an infection has on the body, such as a fever (raised body temperature) or a rash, are called the symptoms. Different microorganisms cause different symptoms, but they all damage the body in one way or another. The damage is done to the body's cells.

2) Some microorganisms damage cells directly. For example, malaria parasites invade red blood cells and destroy their haemoglobin (the substance used to carry oxygen), eventually making the cells burst open. Malaria causes flu-like symptoms.

3) Many microorganisms produce chemicals that damage cells. Some bacteria produce enzymes that break down the material holding cells together. This helps the bacteria to invade the body more deeply. One example is the very common Staphylococcus bacteria that can infect wounds or cause food poisoning.

4) The chemicals made by many bacteria are called toxins. They poison cells, causing fever or inflammation (painful swelling). Some strains of Escherichia coli cause diarrhoea by secreting toxic substances.

Your Body Has Barriers to Keep Microorganisms Out

Fortunately, it's not very easy for microorganisms to get into your body and start causing havoc. Your body has some pretty nifty defence systems in place:

1) The skin is a really effective barrier for keeping microorganisms out. If the skin is damaged, it can rapidly repair itself to stop wounds from getting infected.

2) The skin does contain tiny openings so that sweat can come out to cool you down. Luckily sweat contains substances that reduce the growth of microorganisms. It forms an extra protective layer over the skin.

3) Your eyes produce tears, which contain enzymes that can kill bacteria.

4) Bacteria that enter your body in food or drink usually get killed by the hydrochloric acid in your stomach. This stops them from spreading through your body.

Don't wash — fight disease using sweat alone (yummy)...

The key things that you must get into your head from this page are:
Microorganisms spread rapidly, they cause symptoms by damaging cells, and your body has ways of keeping them out. Make sure you've learnt all the little details too and you'll be fine.

The Immune System

From time to time microorganisms <u>do</u> make it past your outer defences and into the body. But all is not lost, your body still has a pretty powerful weapon left — your <u>white blood cells</u>.

Your Immune System Fights Off Invading Microbes

The role of the <u>immune system</u> is to deal with any pathogens that enter the body. An immune response <u>always</u> involves <u>white blood cells</u>. There are several <u>different types</u> and they all have different jobs to do.

1) Anything that gets into the body should be picked up straight away by a certain type of white blood cell.

2) These white blood cells are able to detect things that are '<u>foreign</u>' to the body, e.g. microorganisms.

3) They then <u>engulf</u> the microbes and <u>digest them</u>.

4) These white blood cells are <u>non-specific</u> — they attack <u>anything</u> that's not meant to be there.

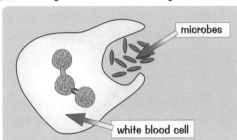

5) The white blood cells also trigger an <u>inflammatory response</u>. <u>Blood flow</u> to the infected area is <u>increased</u> (making the area <u>red</u> and <u>hot</u>), and fluid leaks into the damaged tissue (which makes the area <u>swell up</u>) — this is all so that the right cells can get to the area to <u>fight</u> the infection.

Antibodies Recognise Foreign Microorganisms

A different group of white blood cells attack <u>specific</u> microorganisms.

1) These white blood cells have receptors that recognise particular <u>antigens</u>. Antigens are substances that trigger <u>immune responses</u> — they're usually <u>protein</u> molecules on the surface of a <u>microorganism</u> cell.

2) Certain kinds of white blood cell produce <u>antibodies</u>. Antibodies are proteins that are <u>specific</u> to a particular antigen — a different one is needed to recognise each different microorganism.

3) Antibodies <u>latch onto</u> invading microorganisms and do one of three things:

- They <u>mark</u> the microorganism so other <u>white blood cells</u> can engulf and digest it.
- They bind to and <u>neutralise</u> viruses or toxins.
- Some can even attach to bacteria and <u>kill them directly</u>.

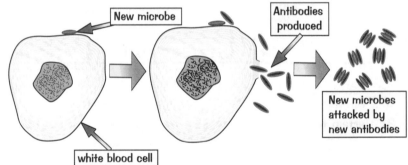

4) Once the <u>right white blood cell</u> recognises the antigens on a microorganism, it <u>divides</u> to make <u>more identical cells</u> which make lots of the right <u>antibody</u> to get on with fighting the infection.

5) Some white blood cells stay around in the blood after the original infection has been fought off. They can reproduce very quickly if the <u>same</u> antigen enters the body for a <u>second</u> time.

6) That's why you're immune to <u>most</u> diseases that you've already had — the body carries a "<u>memory</u>" of what the antigen was like, and can quickly produce loads of antibodies if you get infected again.

White blood cells are pretty handy...

Have you ever noticed that loads of people seem to get <u>colds</u> as soon as they come back to school after the <u>summer holidays</u>? The reason is that people have been away on <u>holiday</u> and brought back new microorganisms that most people don't have the <u>antibodies</u> for.

Vaccination

Some diseases can be pretty nasty, so if possible you want to give your immune system a
head start in fighting the microorganisms that cause it. You can do this using a vaccine.

Vaccinations Use a Safe Version of a Dangerous Microorganism

1) When you're infected with a new
microorganism, it takes your white blood cells
a few days to get their numbers up and to
make the right antibodies to help them deal
with it. By that time, you can get pretty ill.

2) Immunisation involves injecting dead or
inactive microorganisms. These still carry
the same antigens, which means your body
produces antibodies to attack them —
even though the microorganism is harmless
(since it's dead or inactive).

3) For example, the MMR vaccine contains
weakened versions of the viruses that
cause measles, mumps and rubella
(German measles) all together.

4) If live microorganisms of the same type
appear after that, the white blood cells can
rapidly mass-produce antibodies to kill off
the pathogen.

5) This normally means you can get rid of the
disease-causing microorganisms before they
reach a level that makes you sick.

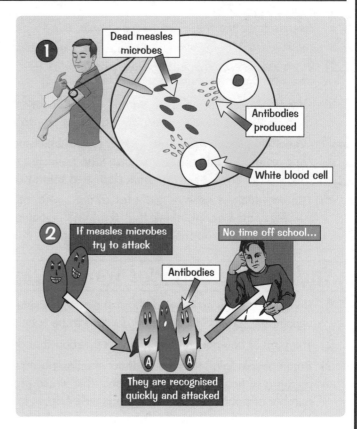

Some Microorganisms Change Very Quickly

1) When microorganisms reproduce, their DNA sometimes changes too.
This is called mutation and it's totally random.

2) These changes to the DNA can alter the structure and characteristics of the microorganisms.

3) Certain types of microorganism tend to mutate often. This makes it hard to develop vaccines for these
kinds of microorganisms, because the changes to their DNA can lead to them having different antigens.

4) The virus that causes influenza (flu) is one kind of microorganism that mutates very quickly.
New vaccines against new strains of influenza have to be developed on a regular basis.

5) There can be other reasons why vaccination is difficult. The HIV virus that causes AIDS actually
attacks some of your white blood cells. Only certain kinds of white blood cell are affected,
but it's enough to stop the immune system from working properly — and so the impact of a vaccine is
limited. To make matters worse, the HIV virus is another microorganism that has a high mutation rate.

The first ever vaccine was invented by a cow...

Well, sort of. Edward Jenner is usually credited with giving the first vaccine in 1796. He infected a boy
with cowpox, a cow disease that causes only mild symptoms in humans. The antigens on the virus were
similar enough to those on the human smallpox virus for antibodies against smallpox to be made, making
the boy immune to it. However, Jenner only got the idea when he noticed that cow farmers rarely got
smallpox (because they'd already caught cowpox), so I think we should just credit the cows.

Vaccination Pros and Cons

Even if you <u>can</u> give a person a vaccine to prevent a disease, not everyone thinks you necessarily <u>should</u>...

There are <u>Pros</u> and <u>Cons</u> of Vaccination

PROS

1) Big outbreaks of diseases — called <u>epidemics</u> — can be prevented if a <u>large percentage</u> of the population is vaccinated. That way, even the people who aren't vaccinated are unlikely to catch the disease because there are fewer people able to pass it on. But if a significant number of people <u>aren't</u> vaccinated, the disease can <u>spread</u> quickly through them and lots of people will be ill at the same time.

2) Some diseases, such as <u>smallpox</u>, have been virtually <u>wiped out</u> by vaccination programmes.

CONS

1) Vaccinations can <u>never</u> be <u>completely safe</u> for everyone, because individual immune systems will have <u>different reactions</u> to the vaccine.

2) Vaccines sometimes cause <u>side effects</u>, which are worse in some people than in others. For example, one in four children who have the <u>meningitis vaccination</u> develop a painful <u>swelling</u> at the site of the injection, and one in 50 have a <u>fever</u> after the vaccine.

3) Some vaccines have raised a lot of concerns, but their possible side effects have never been <u>proved</u> — e.g. some people think that the <u>MMR vaccination</u> increases the risk of developing <u>autism</u> (a condition that affects how people understand the world around them and communicate with others).

Individuals <u>May Not Want</u> to Do What's Best for <u>Society</u>

1) Some people are so worried about the possible side effects of some vaccines that they <u>refuse</u> to be vaccinated, or won't allow their children to be vaccinated.

2) There must be enough people in a population that <u>do</u> get vaccinated if the disease is to be <u>controlled</u>.

3) Some people think that the right vaccination policy would be the one that leads to the <u>best outcome</u> for the <u>majority</u> of people in the population. This would probably mean ensuring that <u>everyone</u> is vaccinated, as the number of people who suffer <u>serious</u> side effects is likely to be far <u>less</u> than the number of people <u>protected</u> from the serious effects of diseases like measles and rubella.

4) Another argument is that it's <u>unfair</u> for some people to avoid all risk by refusing to be vaccinated, because they still <u>benefit</u> from living in a society where most people <u>are</u> vaccinated. They're unlikely to catch the disease because there's no-one to pass it on to them — everyone else has risked having the vaccine.

5) The reverse argument is that nobody should be <u>forced</u> to have a vaccination that they don't want — each person should have the <u>right</u> to decide about vaccination for themselves and their children.

6) This is one possible example of the important distinction between what is <u>technically possible</u> (e.g. vaccinating every person in the UK) and what is <u>right</u> (e.g. allowing people the freedom to decide their own actions). Some people believe that certain actions are <u>never</u> justified, even if they do benefit the majority, because they're unnatural or wrong — but not everyone agrees on what these actions are.

7) In <u>richer</u> developed countries there's usually enough money available to vaccinate <u>everyone</u> who agrees to it. This is why the <u>majority</u> of children in the UK <u>are</u> routinely vaccinated against diseases such as measles, mumps and rubella.

8) In <u>poorer</u> developing countries there might <u>not</u> be enough money to vaccinate everyone, so vaccination programmes are followed that vaccinate certain people in a way that <u>best controls</u> the disease. This could be done by vaccinating just people living on the <u>edge</u> of a community, to stop the disease spreading outwards.

"It won't hurt"
— yeah right.

Come on, let meee–eeeeee... vaccinate yoooouu...

After all the <u>controversy</u> about the MMR vaccine, a lot of parents thought that it wasn't worth the <u>risk</u> just to prevent measles, mumps and rubella. But these illnesses can be <u>more serious</u> than you might think — even in rich, developed countries, 0.3% of children who catch measles <u>die</u> due to complications like pneumonia. An even greater percentage die in developing countries.

Antibiotics

The discovery of the first <u>antibiotic</u>, penicillin, was a huge one in medicine — suddenly infections that had often been fatal could be <u>cured</u>. But unfortunately antibiotics may <u>not</u> be a permanent solution.

Antibiotics Can Kill Bacteria and Fungi, but Not Viruses

1) <u>Antibiotics</u> are drugs that can kill <u>bacteria</u> and <u>fungi</u> without seriously damaging your own body cells.

2) They're very useful for clearing up infections that your own immune system is having <u>trouble</u> with.

3) However, they <u>don't kill viruses</u>. <u>Flu and colds</u> are caused by <u>viruses</u> and basically you just have to <u>wait</u> for your body to deal with them and <u>suffer</u> in the meantime. <u>HIV</u> is a virus too, which is why there's <u>no cure</u>.

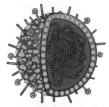

A horrid Flu Virus

Bacteria Can Evolve and Become Antibiotic-Resistant...

1) Like all organisms, microorganisms sometimes develop <u>random mutations</u> in their DNA.

2) These can lead to changes in the microorganism's characteristics. Sometimes, they mean that the organism is <u>less affected</u> by a particular <u>antibiotic</u>.

3) For the microorganism, this ability to resist antibiotics is a big <u>advantage</u>. It's better able to survive, even in a host who's being treated to get rid of the infection, and so it lives for longer and <u>reproduces</u> many more times.

4) This leads to the <u>gene</u> for resistance being <u>passed on</u> to lots of offspring — it's just <u>natural selection</u> (see page 69). This is how it spreads and becomes <u>more common</u> in a population of microorganisms.

5) This is a problem for people who become infected with these microorganisms, because you <u>can't</u> easily get rid of them with antibiotics. Sometimes drug companies can come up with a <u>new</u> antibiotic that's effective, but '<u>superbugs</u>' that are resistant to most known antibiotics are becoming more common.

...So Do Everyone a Favour and Always Finish Your Antibiotics

1) The <u>more</u> antibiotics are used, the <u>bigger</u> the problem of antibiotic-resistance becomes. Although the antibiotic might get rid of most of the bacteria or fungi, there's always the danger that a few of the <u>most antibiotic-resistant</u> ones will be left behind.

2) These can then <u>reproduce</u> to create a <u>whole population</u> of antibiotic-resistant microorganisms. This has happened with the bacteria that cause <u>tuberculosis</u> (TB), making it hard to cure. To cure TB, you need a long course of at least three different antibiotics.

3) In fact, <u>all</u> bacteria <u>vary</u> in their resistance to drugs, and when a disease is treated with antibiotics the most resistant ones are the <u>last</u> to go.

4) This is why it's important you take <u>all</u> the antibiotics a doctor prescribes for you. Lots of people stop bothering to take their antibiotics as soon as they <u>feel better</u>, but that just means that <u>most</u> of the microorganisms are gone. The really <u>hardcore</u> ones could still be lingering on.

5) It's also important that people only use antibiotics when they <u>really</u> need to. It's not that antibiotics actually <u>cause</u> resistance, but they do create a situation where naturally resistant microorganisms have an <u>advantage</u> and so increase in numbers. If they're not actually doing you any good, it's pointless to take antibiotics and it could actually be harmful.

Aaargh, a giant earwig! Run from the attack of the superbug...

The reality of <u>superbugs</u> is possibly even scarier than giant earwigs. Actually, nothing's more scary than giant earwigs, but microorganisms that are <u>resistant</u> to <u>all</u> our drugs are a worrying thought. It'll be like going <u>back in time</u> to before antibiotics were invented. So far <u>new drugs</u> have kept us one step ahead, but some people think it's only a matter of time until the options run out.

Drug Trials

You can't just get any old chemical and market it as a new wonder drug. Any new drug has to go through loads of tests to make sure it's safe to use, and also to make sure it actually does what you claim it does.

Drugs are Tested First in a Laboratory

1) New drugs are being developed all the time to help fight different diseases.

2) Any new drug must be tested to make sure that it's safe to use and that it actually works.

3) The way drug trials are structured aims to weed out potentially harmful substances before they're given to any human volunteers.

4) Any new drug must be tested on at least two different species of live mammal (rats and monkeys are often used) before it's given to humans. Many animals have systems that are similar to those of humans, so the tests give early indications of what the drug might do in the human body. If the drug causes serious problems in the animals, the testing is unlikely to go any further, and this saves any humans from being harmed.

5) Drugs can also be tested on human cells that are grown in the lab. Unlike the animal tests, these tests are measuring the effect on real human cells, which is an advantage. On the other hand they can't recreate the conditions in a whole system or organism.

Drugs are Then Tested on Humans in Clinical Trials

1) If the laboratory tests don't pick up on anything that could limit how useful the drug will be, it will then go on to be tested on human volunteers. These tests are called clinical trials.

2) First, the drug is tested on healthy volunteers. This is to make sure it doesn't have any harmful side effects when the body is working normally. Sick people are likely to be more vulnerable to any damage the drug could do, which is why the drug isn't tested on them yet.

3) If the results of the tests on healthy volunteers are good, the drugs can be tested on people suffering from the illness. These are tests for both safety and effectiveness.

4) Placebos are usually used in human drug trials. These are 'fake' treatments which don't actually involve giving the drug to the patient. This is so you can compare a group of people who were given the actual drug with a group who were given the placebo. In some trials where patients are seriously ill placebos aren't used because it's unethical not to allow all patients to get the potential benefits of the new drug.

5) If the drug is going to be useful, the results should show that the condition of the volunteers in the group given the real drug improved more than those in the group given the placebo. If there are side effects associated with taking the drug, e.g. drowsiness, then the patients in the group taking the real drug will report feeling these more than the patients taking the placebo.

6) Placebos are necessary in both 'blind' and 'double-blind' human trials:

In blind trials, patients don't know if they've been given the drug or a placebo. This is because a patient who knows they're being treated might feel better for psychological reasons, even if there hasn't really been an improvement. In the same way a patient who knows they're not being treated might not feel better even if they are recovering. Blind trials eliminate these effects.

In double-blind trials, even the scientists carrying out the research don't find out until the end which patients got real drugs and which got placebos. This is so the scientists monitoring the patients and analysing the results aren't subconsciously influenced by their knowledge.

Blind trials used to test new eye drops...

You can't know for sure what will happen in a complete human system until you test one. A trial in London in March 2006 left six men seriously ill after a new anti-inflammatory drug caused 'completely unanticipated' effects. But then, if nobody ever took part in trials, there would never be any new drugs.

The Circulatory System

Blood is vital. It moves oxygen from your lungs to your cells, carbon dioxide from your cells to your lungs, food from your gut to your cells, hormones from your glands to your cells... oh, I'm exhausted.

The Heart and Blood Vessels Supply Blood to the Body

1) Blood is circulated around the body in tubes called blood vessels. Oxygen and food are carried in the blood to the body cells, and waste substances such as carbon dioxide are carried away from the cells.

2) The heart is a pumping organ that keeps the blood flowing through the vessels. It's made up of muscle cells that keep it beating continually. These cells need their own blood supply to deliver the food and oxygen needed to keep the heart beating continually.

3) Blood is supplied to the heart by two coronary arteries, which branch from the base of the aorta (the biggest artery in the body).

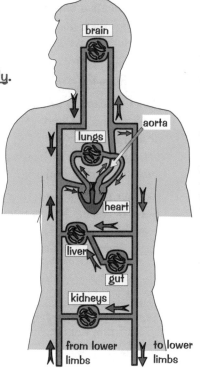

There are two major types of blood vessel

1) Arteries carry oxygenated blood away from the heart to the body cells (including the heart muscle).

2) It comes out of the heart at high pressure, so the artery walls have to be strong and elastic.

3) Look how thick the walls are compared to the size of the hole down the middle (called the lumen).

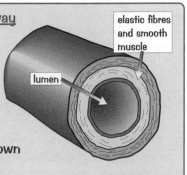

1) Veins carry deoxygenated blood back to the heart.
2) The blood is at a lower pressure in the veins so the walls don't need to be as thick.
3) They have a bigger lumen than arteries, to help the blood flow more easily.
4) They also have valves to help keep the blood flowing in the right direction.

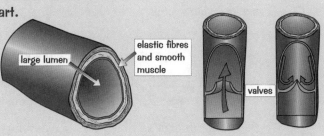

Fatty Deposits Can Cause Problems for the Heart

1) If there's too much fat in the diet, it can enter the blood and build up in the walls of arteries.
2) This makes the lumen of the artery narrower.
3) When this happens in the coronary arteries, it can restrict the flow of blood to the heart's muscle cells.
4) The amount of oxygen that can be supplied to the muscle cells is reduced, so they can't work properly. This can lead to a heart attack.

Unbreak my heart — say it's pumping again...

So in fact, your boyfriend or girlfriend saying they don't want to go out with you any more won't really break your heart, despite what all these warblers on the radio seem to think. Putting on eight stone in weight through comforting yourself with ice cream might do it though.

Heart Disease

You know from earlier in the section that loads of <u>diseases</u> are caused by nasty <u>microorganisms</u> that sneak into the body. But this <u>isn't</u> usually the case with <u>heart disease</u>.

Lifestyle Factors <u>Can Increase the Risk</u> of Heart Disease

1) Heart disease can often be linked to <u>lifestyle factors</u>, such as what someone <u>eats</u> and how much <u>exercise</u> they do. Some people might be more at risk because of their <u>genes</u> too. In most people it's a condition caused by one or both of these things, rather than by microorganisms.

2) The main lifestyle factors that increase the risk of heart disease are a <u>high-fat diet</u>, <u>stress</u>, <u>smoking</u>, and too much <u>alcohol</u>.

3) Heart disease is more common in <u>industrialised countries</u>, such as the UK and USA, than in non-industrialised countries. This is mainly because people in these countries can <u>afford</u> a lot of high-fat food and often don't <u>need</u> to be very physically active.

bad bad bad

good good good

4) <u>Regular moderate exercise</u> reduces the risk of developing heart disease. This is because exercise <u>burns fat</u>, preventing it building up in the arteries. Exercise also <u>strengthens</u> the heart muscle.

Epidemiological Studies <u>Can Identify Possible</u> Risk Factors

<u>Epidemiology</u> is the study of <u>patterns</u> of disease, the factors that affect the <u>spread</u> of disease, and why some groups of people are more <u>likely</u> to get certain illnesses than others.

1) For example, studies into the <u>epidemiology</u> of <u>heart disease</u> have shown which factors are most likely to cause the disease.

2) People who <u>smoke</u> more have been shown to suffer more from heart disease, so there's said to be a <u>correlation</u> between smoking and heart disease (see next page).

3) As with all scientific studies, epidemiological studies are more convincing if they're based on <u>lots</u> of cases. Single cases <u>don't</u> provide good evidence for or against a correlation.

4) Scientific studies can only be considered <u>reliable</u> once they've been <u>peer reviewed</u>. This means that they're evaluated by <u>other scientists</u> (their peers) before the claims are widely accepted. The methods and results are published in <u>scientific journals</u>, so that anyone can read them and make up their own mind. Some scientists might decide to carry out <u>similar studies</u> to see if their results agree, and some might come up with <u>alternative explanations</u> for the results.

5) It usually takes a lot of discussion, argument and further studies before a new idea becomes accepted. This is generally a good thing — there are often lots of <u>different</u> ways to explain a set of data, and just because someone's done the research it doesn't mean they'll automatically pick the <u>right</u> one.

Usually it's peer review, occasionally it's handbags at dawn...

Scientists through the ages have come up with some <u>amazing theories</u>, but they have also often acted like great big kids. <u>Stealing</u> one another's ideas, taking <u>credit</u> for other people's work, <u>fixing</u> their results, even occasionally resorting to <u>physical violence</u> to settle an intellectual dispute. Dear oh dear.

Correlation and Cause

It takes a long time for any new scientific discovery to become accepted. And here's why...

Statistical Correlations Don't Prove One Thing Causes Another

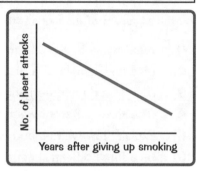

No. of heart attacks

Years after giving up smoking

1) A correlation is basically just a relationship between two factors. For example, say scientists monitored the number of heart attacks in a group of ex-smokers. If they got results like those shown on the right, this would indicate that there's a negative correlation between these two factors — the longer people in this study group had given up for, the less likely they were to have a heart attack.

2) Most scientific studies aim to work out whether there's a correlation between two factors. But you have to be careful, because a correlation doesn't necessarily mean that one thing causes the other.

3) For example, many people suffering from high blood pressure also have joint problems. However, the high blood pressure doesn't actually cause the joint problems.

4) There's also a correlation between high blood pressure and body weight, and in this case being overweight does cause the high blood pressure. Being overweight causes joint problems too, which is why blood pressure and joint problems seem to be correlated. This is often the real reason that two factors show a correlation — some other factor is linking the two.

Scientific Studies Must Be Carefully Planned

A lot of different things can affect how reliable the results of a study are. And I mean a whole lot...

1) When studying the relationship between two variables, scientists need to consider all the other things that could be contributing to the outcome they're interested in. For example, a study looking at how smoking affects the risk of heart disease would need to take into account many other factors too — things like the body weight of the people in the study and the amount of exercise they do could also affect their risk of heart disease.

2) Studies like this must try to minimise the effects of these other factors. The study should use volunteers who have similar body weights and who do similar levels of exercise. This doesn't mean that all the people have to be the same weight, but that the average weight of the two groups, smokers and non-smokers, should be as similar as possible.

3) A study into the effect of smoking on heart disease should also look at as many people as possible. This reduces the chance of any unusual results (called anomalies) affecting the overall pattern. The more people (or lab rats, or bananas, or repetitions of the experiment) there are in a study, the more reliable it's likely to be.

4) This is why, when people say things like "My gran smoked 60 cigarettes a day since she was 12 and lived to be 90," it doesn't actually mean cigarettes are harmless. There are always going to be unusual results that happen by chance. One individual case doesn't prove anything at all — you need a big sample to be able to show a significant correlation.

5) You can be more confident that a factor affects the outcome if you can also think of a mechanism to explain why. E.g. a high fat diet can increase your blood pressure. That's because more fat builds up in the walls of your arteries, making it more difficult for blood to get through them.

6) It's also important that results are repeatable by other scientists. They're more likely to be reliable if other scientists who carry out a similar study get the same results. If they don't, there must be some reason why — the experiment was flawed, or the results were a random one-off.

I think there's a correlation between high BP and this page...

OCR like to talk about factors and outcomes in scientific studies. Don't be put off — the outcome is just the variable you're measuring, e.g. amount of heart disease, and there will be various factors that affect it.

Revision Summary for Module B2

Another section, another revision summary, in much the same way that night follows day. Now, as you answer these questions you can take part in a little experiment. My theory is that the number of questions you can answer correctly without looking back through the section depends on your star sign. Have a go and then see if your score matches my predictions at the bottom of the page. (Which are based on the alignment of the moon with Jupiter and whether or not I like the sound of the star sign name.)

1) What name is given to microorganisms that cause disease?

2) Give an example of a disease where the symptoms are caused by direct damage to the cells.

3) How else do microorganisms produce symptoms?

4) Give three different ways that your body is adapted to keep microorganisms out.

5) Explain how white blood cells help to get rid of microorganisms that do enter the body.

6) Give three different ways that antibodies help to get rid of an infection.

7) Explain why you are immune to most diseases that you've already had.

8)* Vaccination involves injecting inactive microbes. How does this give you immunity in the future?

9) Which three diseases can be prevented by having the MMR vaccine?

10) Vaccines against the flu are different every year. Why is this?

11) Explain why scientists have not yet been able to produce a vaccine against the HIV virus.

12) What do some people think is a possible (though unproven) side effect of the MMR vaccine?

13) In 1993, 95% of children had the MMR vaccine. How would this also benefit the 5% who didn't?

14)* Describe how fears about the side effects of a vaccine could potentially lead to an epidemic.

15) Explain how the vaccination programmes of developed and developing countries might differ.

16) What is an antibiotic?

17) Explain why antibiotics should not be prescribed for someone with the flu.

18) What is a 'superbug'?

19) Why are patients advised to complete a course of antibiotics even if they start to feel better?

20) Give two ways that new drugs are usually tested before they're given to humans.

21) Why are new drugs tested on healthy people first, not patients with the illness they're designed for?

22) Explain what a placebo is.

23) What is a double-blind trial?

24) Name the blood vessels that supply blood to the heart.

25) How is the structure of an artery adapted to its function?

26) How is the structure of a vein adapted to its function?

27) Explain how a diet high in fat can cause a heart attack.

28) Your lifestyle can increase your risk of heart disease. What else can increase your risk?

29) Give the four main lifestyle factors associated with an increased risk of heart disease.

30) Why is heart disease more common in industrialised countries?

31) Explain how peer review increases the reliability of scientific studies.

32) Explain why a correlation between two factors doesn't necessarily mean one causes the other.

33) How do scientists minimise the effects of factors other than those they're studying?

34) Why should an epidemiological study include as many patients as possible?

35) Why is a study considered less reliable if the results are not repeatable by other scientists?

PREDICTIONS: Aries 25–29. Taurus 20–24. Gemini 35 or more. Cancer 15–19. Leo 20–24. Virgo 15–19. Libra 30–34. Scorpio 35 or more. Sagittarius 20–24. Capricorn 25–29. Aquarius 35 or more. Pisces — you haven't even tried them yet! Get on with it!

* Answers on page 104.

Natural and Synthetic Materials

This section is all about <u>materials</u>, their <u>properties</u> and the best ones to use to make different <u>products</u>.

All Materials are Made up of Chemicals

Absolutely everything is made up of <u>chemicals</u>.
Chemicals are made up of <u>atoms</u> or <u>groups of atoms</u> bonded together.

1) Iron is a <u>chemical element</u> — it's made up of <u>iron atoms</u>.

2) Water is a <u>chemical</u>. It's made up of lots of <u>water molecules</u>. A molecule is a group of atoms <u>bonded</u> together. Water molecules contain <u>2 chemical elements</u> — hydrogen and oxygen.

Some of These Materials Occur Naturally...

A lot of the materials that we use are made by other <u>living things</u>, not by man:

MATERIALS FROM PLANTS

1) <u>Wood</u> and <u>paper</u> are both made from <u>trees</u>.
2) <u>Cotton</u> comes from the cotton plant.

MATERIALS FROM ANIMALS

1) <u>Wool</u> comes from <u>sheep</u>.
2) <u>Silk</u> is made by the <u>silkworm</u> larva.
3) <u>Leather</u> comes from <u>cows</u>.

...Others are Synthetic — Made by Humans

We often use <u>man-made</u> (synthetic) materials instead of <u>natural</u> materials, e.g.

1) All <u>rubber</u> used to come from the sap of the <u>rubber tree</u>. We <u>still</u> get a lot of rubber this way (e.g. for car tyres), but you can also make rubber in a <u>factory</u>. The advantage of this is that you can <u>control</u> its <u>properties</u>, making it suitable for different <u>purposes</u>, e.g. wetsuits.

2) A lot of <u>clothes</u> are made of <u>man-made</u> materials like <u>nylon</u> or polyester. These materials are often a lot <u>cheaper</u> and have more <u>uses</u> than the natural materials like wool and silk — you can make fabrics that are super-stretchy, or sparkly.

3) <u>Paint</u> is a mixture of man-made chemicals. The <u>pigment</u> (the colouring) and the stuff that holds it all together (the <u>binder</u>) are designed to be <u>tough</u> and to stop the colour fading.

So silk comes out of a worm's bottom then...

OK so now you should know what a <u>material</u> is (and that it doesn't just mean <u>fabric</u>). You should also have a pretty good idea of the different kinds of materials around, and where they come from. Not bad for the first page of the section. Time to cover the page and <u>scribble</u> down what you can remember.

Materials and Properties

Not all materials are the same, as you'll find out if you try to make a hat out of spaghetti hoops...

Different Materials Have Different Properties...

Melting Point

Most materials have a unique melting point. This is the temperature where the solid material turns to liquid.
E.g. the melting point of water is 0 degrees Celsius (0 °C).

Strength

Strength is how good a material is at resisting a force. You can judge how strong it is by how much force is needed to either break it or permanently change its shape (deform it).
There are two types of strength you need to know about:

1) TENSILE (OR TENSION) STRENGTH — how much a material can resist a pulling force.
   Things like ropes and cables need a high tensile strength, or they'd snap.
2) COMPRESSIVE STRENGTH — how much a material can resist a pushing force.
   Aircraft bodies need good compressive strength, or they'd be squashed by the force of the air pushing on them.

Some things, like cross beams in roofs, need to be made of materials with good compressive and tensile strength — they get both pushed and pulled.

Stiffness

A stiff material is good at resisting a temporary change of shape. This is not the same as strength, where the material resists a permanent change.
1) Materials like steel are very difficult to bend — they're very stiff.
2) Some kinds of rubber are very strong but they still bend and stretch very easily — they're not stiff.

Hardness

The hardness of a material is how difficult it is to cut into.

1) The hardest material found in nature is diamond.
2) The only material that can cut a diamond is another diamond.
3) Diamonds can cut most other materials — many industrial drills have diamond tips.

Density

Density is a material's mass per unit volume (e.g. g/cm³). Don't confuse density with mass or weight.

1) Air is not very dense. You'd need a huge volume of it to make up 1 kg in mass.
2) Gold is very dense. A small volume of gold would make up 1 kg in mass.
3) Objects that are less dense than water will float (like ice). Objects that are more dense than water will sink.

Substance	Density g/cm³
gold	19.3
iron	7.21
PVC	1.3
water	1.0
ice	0.97
air	0.001

'Cos diamonds are an industrial drill's best friend...

Learn everything on this page — I make that five things. And make sure you're clear about what density is and why it's NOT the same as mass. Measure out 1 kg of loose change (or rocks) and 1 kg of breakfast cereal and compare the different volumes — same mass, but very different densities...

Making Measurements

When you measure the properties of a material you can only accept the results as reliable if other scientists elsewhere can get a similar result — your experiment has to be repeatable.

Most Measurements Involve a Degree of Uncertainty

When you're measuring something there are loads of reasons why your results might not be accurate:

1) There might be a fault in your equipment.

2) Wrong results can be because of human error — inaccurate measuring, reading or recording of the results.

3) Your samples and techniques have to be the same every time. If lots of scientists all test the strength of iron they might all get different results because iron's strength depends on how it's made and how old it is. The scientists need to work on an identical sample using identical techniques.

Measurements Will Always Vary to Some Extent

If you want an accurate result you've got to take measurements several times. You won't get exactly the same measurement each time, but that's normal. If you want it to be a really accurate value you've got to carry out several tests.

This table shows the results of an experiment to measure the density of gold — the measurement was repeated 10 times:

Test	Density of gold g/cm³
A	19.3
B	19.4
C	12.8
D	19.1
E	30.1
F	19.2
G	19.5
H	19.2
I	19.2
J	19.5

1) The results of tests C and E are so different from the others that something must have gone wrong. Results like these that are an abnormal distance from the rest of the data are called outliers, and you can often just ignore them.

2) Working out what to ignore can be tricky — you need to prove that there's a 'real difference' between the measurements before you can ignore them. Plotting the results on a graph can help with this — you can draw a 'line of best fit' and ignore the results that aren't near it.

3) You can't always ignore outliers — if you're expecting the data to vary a lot, e.g. if you're measuring the height of children aged 1 to 10, then you wouldn't ignore a very low or high result.

4) The table suggests that the true value of the density of gold is in the range of 19.1 – 19.5 g/cm³, where most of the measurements lie.

5) A mean (average) gives you the best estimate of the true value. Take a mean of the remaining results (add them together then divide by the number of good results (8)). This works out at 19.3 g/cm³.

Experiments Need to be Carefully Designed

1) Measuring a mean and ignoring outliers isn't enough. You also need to make sure that your experiment is a fair test.

2) The best way to make it a fair test is to vary only one factor in your experiment, and to only measure one thing at a time.

3) So if you're measuring densities of different materials, the only thing that you should vary each time should be the material — that's the factor that you change. The volume of material that you test, the temperature and equipment that you use etc. must all be exactly the same each time.

4) Each time you repeat the test the other factors must be exactly the same — they must be controlled.

I'm studying for a degree of uncertainty right now...

This page is mostly about making sure that measurements are accurate, but it applies to any kind of scientific test really. If you don't follow these rules, then you can't really conclude anything from your results. These rules have to be followed by everyone, even the top scientists — so learn them now.

Materials, Properties and Uses

Every material has a <u>different</u> set of properties, which makes it <u>perfect</u> for some jobs, and totally <u>useless</u> for others. That probably explains why <u>chocolate teapots</u> have never really caught on...

The Possible Uses for a Material Depend on its Properties

When you're choosing a material to use in a <u>product</u>, you need to think about its <u>properties</u>, e.g.

<u>PLASTICS</u>
- Can be fairly <u>hard</u>, strong and <u>stiff</u>
- Some are fairly <u>low density</u> (good for lightweight goods)
- Some are <u>mouldable</u> (easily made into things)

E.g. televisions, computers, kettles

<u>RUBBER</u>
- <u>Strong</u> but soft and <u>flexible</u>
- <u>Mouldable</u>

E.g. rubber car tyres

<u>NYLON FIBRES</u>
- Soft and flexible
- Good <u>tensile strength</u>

E.g. ropes and clothing fabric

A Product's Properties Depend on the Materials It's Made From

Some products can be made from a <u>variety</u> of materials. How <u>good</u> the product is and how long it <u>lasts</u> depends on the <u>properties</u> of the materials it's made from.

1) <u>Gramophone records</u> 100 years ago were made of a <u>mixture</u> of natural materials like paper, slate and wax. There aren't many of these records left because they <u>broke</u> very easily — they weren't <u>flexible</u>.

2) More <u>modern</u> records are made of <u>Poly Vinyl Chloride (PVC)</u> or "<u>vinyl</u>". This material is <u>strong</u> but <u>flexible</u> so it is less likely to break. DJs sometimes still use vinyl records in clubs.

3) Most people these days own <u>Compact Discs (CDs)</u>. These are made of a very <u>tough</u>, <u>flexible</u> plastic called <u>polycarbonate</u>. It's quite strong and hard (it's used in bulletproof glass) and should last <u>even longer</u> than PVC — but we'll have to wait a while to find out...

You'll Need to Assess the Suitability of Different Materials

You need to be able to look at the <u>properties</u> of a material and work out what sort of <u>purposes</u> it might be <u>suitable</u> for, e.g.

1) <u>Cooking utensils</u> must be made from something with a <u>high melting point</u> that's <u>non-toxic</u>.

2) Material to make a <u>toy car</u> must be <u>non-toxic</u> and be <u>strong</u>, <u>stiff</u> and <u>low density</u> — e.g. some kinds of plastic.

3) <u>Clothing fabric</u> mustn't be stiff, but needs a <u>good tensile strength</u> (so it can be made into fibres) and high <u>flame resistance</u> if it's for nightwear or children's clothes.

It's not rocket science — that's 'cos it's materials science...

It's all fairly <u>straightforward</u> stuff on this page — just be prepared to look at the properties of 'mystery' materials in the exam, and work out which material would be <u>most suitable</u> for different jobs. Don't think that any of the materials are totally useless — their properties will probably be <u>ideal</u> for something.

Chemical Synthesis

Crude oil is formed from the buried remains of plants and animals — it's a fossil fuel. Over millions of years, with high temperature and pressure, the remains turn to crude oil, which can be drilled up.

Crude Oil is a Mixture of Lots of Substances

1) Crude oil is a mixture of hydrocarbons — molecules which are made of chains of carbon and hydrogen. (see p.18 for more info).

2) Each hydrocarbon has a chain of a different length. As the length of the carbon chain changes, the properties of the hydrocarbon change. Short chain molecules have lower boiling points — they're often gases. Long chain molecules have high boiling points and can be quite viscous (thick and sticky).

Crude Oil Has Various Uses

Crude oil is pretty useless on its own, but if you separate the mixture you get loads of useful things. The hydrocarbons are sorted into groups with other hydrocarbons that have chains of similar length. This process is called refining.

The uses of a hydrocarbon depend on the length of its molecule chains:

1) Refinery gas has a short chain (3 carbons) — it's a gas at room temperature. This makes it ideal for bottled (camping) gas.

2) Petrol has a longer chain (8 carbons). It's a liquid that flows easily from a car fuel tank to the engine.

3) Bitumen (about 40 carbons) is very viscous — it's used for covering roads. Other long-chain hydrocarbons are used as lubricants, e.g. engine oil.

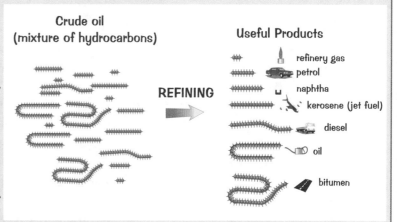

Crude Oil is Used to Make Loads of Synthetic Substances

1) Most of the hydrocarbons in crude oil are used for fuel.

2) Only a very small amount of hydrocarbons from crude oil are chemically modified to make new compounds for use in things like plastics, medicines, fertilisers and even food.

3) Some of the less useful hydrocarbons can be split apart to make more useful hydrocarbons and ethene, which is really useful for making plastics. This process is called cracking.

long-chain hydrocarbon molecule, e.g. kerosene (10 C atoms) → octane (8 C atoms) (useful for petrol) + ethene (for making plastics)

Crude oil — it's always cracking dirty jokes...

It's amazing what you get from buried dead stuff. But it has had a few hundred million years to get into the useful state it's in now. So if we use it all we're going to have to wait an awfully long time for more to form. No one knows when it'll run out, but some scientists think it'll only last another 30 years.

Polymerisation

Polymers are one of the most important man-made materials — you can make loads of useful stuff from them — well, as long as you want a plastic-type thing, anyway. And I often do.

Polymerisation Means Loads of Small Molecules Link Together

1) Plastics are formed when lots of small molecules called monomers join together to give a polymer.

2) They're usually carbon based.

3) Under high pressure many small molecules "join hands" (polymerise) to form long saturated chains called polymers.

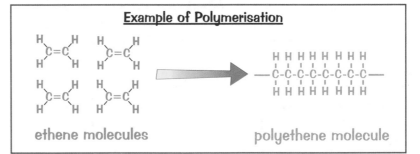

Example of Polymerisation

ethene molecules → polyethene molecule

Different Polymers Have Different Properties

Different polymers have different physical properties — some are stronger, some are stretchier, some are more easily moulded, and so on. These different physical properties make them suited for different uses.

- Strong, rigid polymers such as high density polyethene are used to make plastic milk bottles.

- Light, stretchable polymers such as low density polyethene are used for plastic bags and squeezy bottles. Low density polyethene has a low melting point, so it's no good for anything that'll get very hot.

- PVC is strong and durable, and it can be made either rigid or stretchy. The rigid kind is used to make window frames and piping. The stretchy kind is used to make synthetic leather.

- Polystyrene foam is used in packaging to protect breakable things, and it's used to make disposable coffee cups (the trapped air in the foam makes it a brilliant thermal insulator).

- Heat-resistant polymers such as melamine resin and polypropene are used to make plastic kettles.

Polymers Have Replaced Natural Materials for Some Uses

Polymers have been used as alternatives to traditional materials in loads of applications:

1) Fizzy drinks bottles are usually made from polymer (plastic). They're often made of a polymer called PET, which is a form of polyester.

2) Fizzy drinks used to come in glass bottles. Glass is made from natural materials. It's more dense than PET and it shatters if you drop it.

3) The new PET bottles are less dense, so they're easier and cheaper to transport.

4) They're also safer, because they don't break easily.

5) PET is recyclable, just like glass. The polymers can be broken down and reformed.

Revision — it's all about stringing lots of facts together...

If you're making a product, you need to pick your plastic carefully. It's no good making a kettle from plastic that melts at 50 °C — you'll end up with a messy kitchen, a burnt hand and no cuppa. You'd also have a bit of difficulty trying to wear clothes made of brittle, unbendy plastic.

Structures and Properties of Polymers

You need to know how the properties of a polymer are affected by the way it's made.

A Polymer's Properties Decide its Uses...

...And its Properties Depend on How the Molecules are Arranged...

The long chain molecules that make up polymers also determine the polymer's properties. How the chains are arranged has a lot to do with it:

> If the polymer chains are packed close together, the material will have a high density.
> If the polymer chains are spread out, the material will have a low density.

...And How They're Held Together

The forces between the different chains of the polymer hold it together as a solid mass.

Weak Forces:
Long chains held together by weak forces are free to slide over each other. This means the plastic can be stretched easily, and will have a low melting point.

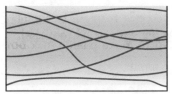

Strong Forces:
Plastics with stronger bonds between the polymer chains have higher melting points and can't be stretched, as the crosslinks hold the chains firmly together.

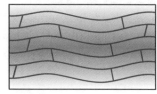

So, the stronger the bonds between the polymer chains, the more energy is needed to break them apart, and the higher the melting point.

Polymers Can be Modified To Give Them Different Properties

You can chemically modify polymers to change their properties.

1) Polymers can be modified to increase their chain length. Polymers with short chains are easy to shape and have lower melting points. Longer chain polymers are stiffer and have higher melting points.

2) Polymers can be made stronger by adding cross-linking agents. These chemicals chemically bond the chains together making the polymer stiffer, stronger and more heat-resistant.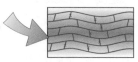

3) Plasticisers can be added to a polymer to make it softer and easier to shape. Plasticisers work by getting in between the polymer chains and reducing the forces between them.

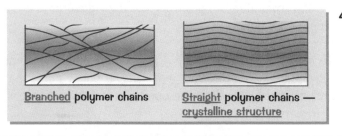

Branched polymer chains   Straight polymer chains — crystalline structure

4) The polymer can be made more crystalline. A crystalline polymer has straight chains with no branches so the chains can fit close together. Crystalline polymers have higher density, are stronger and have a higher melting point.

Choose your polymers wisely...

The molecules that make up a plastic affect the properties of the plastic, which also affects what the plastic can be used for. I know there's a lot of diagrams of lines on this page, but the structure of polymers is really important — it affects their properties, and it might even come up in the exam.

Life Cycle Assessments

If a company wants to manufacture a new product, they carry out a <u>Life Cycle Assessment (LCA)</u>.
This looks at every <u>stage</u> of the product's life to assess the <u>impact</u> it would have on the environment.

Life Cycle Assessments *Show Total Environmental Costs*

A <u>Life Cycle Assessment (LCA)</u> looks at each stage of the life cycle of the product from the <u>raw materials</u> to when it's <u>disposed</u> of, and works out the potential <u>environmental impact</u>:

1) <u>Extracting and refining raw materials</u>

E.g. <u>metals</u> may have to be <u>mined</u> from the ground, then <u>extracted</u> from their ore. Polymers come from crude oil, which has to be <u>drilled</u> and <u>refined</u>. All these things use <u>energy</u>, which usually means burning <u>fossil fuels</u>. Sometimes there's a <u>limited supply</u> of the raw material, too — e.g. oil supplies may run out soon.

2) <u>Manufacturing the product</u>

This often uses a lot of <u>energy</u> and may cause <u>pollution</u> and use other resources — e.g. making a new car uses about 9000 litres of water.

3) <u>Using the product</u>

Just <u>using</u> the finished product can also damage the environment — e.g. an <u>electrical product</u> like a TV uses electricity made from burning <u>fossil fuels</u>.

4) <u>Disposing of the product</u>

When people have finished with the product, it has to be disposed of. It might be <u>incinerated</u> (burnt) which might cause air pollution, or it might go into a <u>landfill site</u>, or be <u>recycled</u>. All these options have an <u>environmental impact</u>.

Life Cycle Assessments are Helpful for *Making Decisions*

An <u>LCA</u> helps you work out the best <u>materials</u> and <u>manufacturing process</u> for your product. If the <u>environmental impact</u> or the <u>cost</u> is too high, you can choose another material or manufacturing process. If it's quite low, you might decide to use the materials for <u>other products</u> too.

The LCA can tell you if it's <u>possible</u> to make a product, and what the environmental impact will be. It <u>can't</u> tell you if you SHOULD make the product though — you have to consider other things when you're making your decision:

1) Making the product will <u>benefit</u> some people, like employees and customers — people need jobs, and some products are <u>essential</u> to their customers, e.g. syringes for diabetes sufferers.

2) Some people may be <u>badly affected</u>, e.g. by land pollution when the product is disposed of, or pollution from the mine where the raw material comes from.

3) Many countries have <u>laws</u> which <u>limit</u> how much impact a company can have on the environment. <u>Poorer countries</u> may really need the money that manufacturing brings in. Their governments are under <u>pressure</u> to be <u>less strict</u> about environmental concerns.

Companies can use the information from an LCA to set up a process which <u>doesn't</u> harm the environment so much that future generations suffer. This is called <u>sustainable development</u>. E.g. a paper company only using wood from forests that are <u>replanted</u> and regrow <u>faster</u> than the company is felling them, and taking steps to <u>protect</u> the wildlife that lives in the forests.

Need exercise? Go life-cycling then...

The <u>environmental cost</u> of a product can vary a lot. If it's something that goes out of date quite quickly, like a computer, then it will have a short life cycle. However, high quality expensive furniture might be kept for a lifetime, and its long life cycle mean it has less impact on the environment.

Revision Summary for Module C2

This section has gone from silk and rubber to crude oil and then onwards to environmental issues.
That's an awful lot to take in in one section. Whether you find this topic easy or hard, interesting or dull,
you've simply got to learn it all before the exam. Try these questions and see how much you really know:

1) Give one example of a chemical element.

2) What's a material?

3) Name a material we use that comes from:

a) plants   b) animals

4) Why do we use both natural and synthetic rubber?

5) What's the difference between compressive and tensile strength?

6) What's the hardest material found in nature?

7) Give a definition of density.

8) You're measuring a material — give three reasons why your results might not be accurate.

9) Why should you always repeat your measurements more than once?

10)* You do an experiment to measure the density of a mystery material. You do the measurement 10
times, and your results (in g/cm^3) are as follows: 8.1, 8.3, 8.1, 3.4, 8.0, 14.2, 8.3, 8.4, 8.0, 8.2.

a) Which results would you discard from your data?*

b) What is the mean density of the mystery material?*

11) How can you ensure that an experiment is a fair test?

12) Name 2 properties of each of the following materials that make them useful in manufacturing:

a) Plastic   b) Rubber   c) Nylon

13)* Name three properties that you'd look for when choosing a material to make a child's dinner bowl.

14) What does crude oil contain?

15) What happens when crude oil is refined?

16) What does 'viscous' mean?

17) Does bottled gas have a short or a long chain molecule?

18) What's the name of the process where hydrocarbons are split apart to form shorter chain
hydrocarbons and ethene?

19) Briefly describe what happens during polymerisation.

20) Give an example of a product where a polymer has replaced a natural material.

21) How does the arrangement of polymer chains affect the density of a material?

22) A polymer is easily stretched and has a low melting point. What can you say about the arrangement
of its molecule chains and the forces holding them together?

23) What would you add to a polymer to make it stiffer and stronger?

24) How do plasticisers work?

25) What are the properties of a crystalline polymer?

26) Name the four main stages considered in a Life Cycle Assessment.

27) Explain why a Life Cycle Assessment can't tell you whether you should make a product or not.

28) Give an example of sustainable development.

* Answers on page 104.

Electromagnetic Radiation

Light, X-rays and microwaves are all the <u>same kind of thing</u>, just quite different. Right, that's clear then.

<u>Light</u> *is a <u>Type of</u> <u>Electromagnetic Radiation</u>*

1) <u>Light</u> is a type of <u>electromagnetic radiation</u> (EM radiation).

2) <u>Radiation</u> is just a <u>transfer of energy</u>. E.g. <u>sunlight</u> is a transfer of energy from the Sun to the Earth.

3) <u>Visible light</u> (the seven colours of the rainbow, from red to violet) is just radiation that our <u>eyes</u> can <u>detect</u>. Radiation that's further along in the 'red' direction is called <u>infrared</u>. Similarly, radiation that's further along in the 'violet' direction is called ultraviolet.

4) There are <u>seven</u> types of radiation altogether, making up the <u>electromagnetic spectrum</u> —

RADIO WAVES	MICRO WAVES	INFRA RED	VISIBLE LIGHT	ULTRA VIOLET	X-RAYS	GAMMA RAYS

Electromagnetic Radiation Transfers *Energy in 'Packets'*

1) All types of <u>electromagnetic radiation</u> transfer <u>energy</u>. For example, you can feel the warmth of the Sun because <u>heat energy</u> is travelling through space as <u>infrared radiation</u>.

2) This energy is delivered as <u>photons</u>. A photon is a tiny 'droplet' or 'packet' of energy (imagine droplets of water from a very 'fine' shower — but made of energy rather than water).

Electromagnetic radiation can also be called electromagnetic <u>waves</u> — as in micro<u>waves</u> and radio <u>waves</u>.

Some Types of EM Radiation <u>Transfer More Energy</u> Than Others

1) Each photon carries a tiny quantity of energy, but <u>not all photons</u> have the <u>same amount</u> of energy. The <u>amount of energy</u> carried by a photon depends on the <u>type of radiation</u>.

2) Photon energy increases as you go along the electromagnetic spectrum. <u>Radio</u> wave photons have <u>least energy</u> and <u>gamma ray</u> photons have <u>most energy</u>:

RADIO WAVES	MICRO WAVES	INFRA RED	VISIBLE LIGHT	ULTRA VIOLET	X-RAYS	GAMMA RAYS

increasing energy →

<u>The Royal Mail — they're good at transferring packets...</u>

Remember that EM radiation is just the <u>transfer of energy</u>, as <u>photons</u>. <u>Visible light</u> is just electromagnetic radiation that we can <u>see</u> — and very pretty it is too. There's nothing special about it though — other creatures 'see' other parts of the spectrum — bees see ultraviolet, for instance.

EM Radiation and Energy

All sorts of objects emit EM radiation. <u>You</u>'re emitting some infrared radiation at this very moment.

EM Radiation is Emitted from a Source...

1) Many objects emit electromagnetic radiation, e.g. the Sun, radio transmitters, mobile phones, etc. Any object that emits radiation is called a <u>source</u>.

2) Once emitted, all types of EM radiation can travel through space (a vacuum). In a vacuum, all EM radiation travels at the same speed — the 'speed of light'.

...And Transmitted, Reflected or Absorbed Somewhere Else

1) When radiation is emitted from a source, it <u>spreads out</u> until it reaches some <u>matter</u> (a substance — like air, glass, walls...). Three things can then happen:

> • The radiation might be <u>transmitted</u> — just <u>keep going</u>, like light passes through glass.
> • It could be <u>reflected</u> — <u>bounce back</u>, like light reflected from a mirror.
> • Or the radiation could be <u>absorbed</u> — like a sunbather absorbing UV rays from the Sun.

2) What happens depends on what the <u>substance</u> is like and the <u>type</u> of radiation.

3) Two or three of these things can happen at the same time. E.g. when sunlight shines on glass a lot of the light is <u>transmitted</u>, but <u>some of it</u> is <u>reflected</u> — so you can check your hair in shop windows.

4) Radiation may be absorbed by objects a long way from the source, e.g. when a <u>parked car</u> warms up in the sunshine:

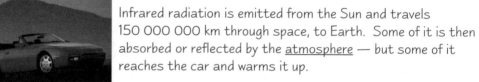

Infrared radiation is emitted from the Sun and travels 150 000 000 km through space, to Earth. Some of it is then absorbed or reflected by the <u>atmosphere</u> — but some of it reaches the car and warms it up.

5) Objects that absorb radiation are called <u>detectors</u> — our <u>eyes</u> are <u>light detectors</u> for instance.

Intensity Decreases as Distance from the Source Increases

1) When radiation is <u>absorbed</u> by matter, the photons <u>transfer their energy</u> to the matter.

2) The energy 'deposited' by a beam of photons depends on <u>how many photons</u> there are and the <u>energy of each photon</u>. (Total energy = number of photons × energy of each photon.)

3) The <u>intensity</u> of radiation means how much <u>energy</u> arrives at <u>each square metre</u> of surface <u>per second</u>.

4) The units of intensity are W/m^2 — <u>watts per square metre</u>.

5) The intensity of a beam of radiation <u>decreases</u> with distance from the source, because the beam spreads out.

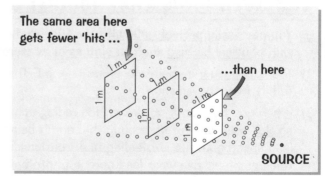

The same area here gets fewer 'hits'...

...than here

SOURCE

6) For example, when you stand near a fire you feel nice and warm. If you moved further away, you'd feel a lot colder — because <u>fewer photons</u> would be reaching you.

Intensity decreases with distance from ketchup...

Remember, <u>different types</u> of EM radiation behave differently. E.g. <u>radio</u> is transmitted through brick walls but light isn't. The other thing to remember from this page is the stuff about <u>intensity</u>. As you get further from the source, intensity decreases. That's why it's cold on Pluto — it's so far from the Sun.

Ionisation

Generally, high-energy EM radiation is more harmful than low-energy radiation. Here's why.

Some EM Radiation Causes Ionisation

1) All substances are made of atoms (see p.89). When a photon hits an atom, it sometimes transfers enough energy to break the atom into bits called ions.

2) This process is called ionisation:

Before ionisation	After ionisation
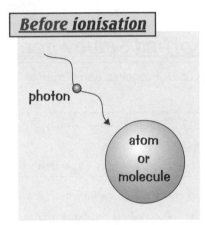	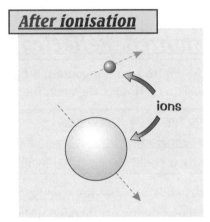

3) It takes a lot of energy to break an atom into ions. So only the higher-energy types of radiation can cause ionisation — ultraviolet, X-rays and gamma rays.

Ionisation is Dangerous if it Happens in Your Cells

1) In the cells in your body, there are many important molecules, including DNA molecules. DNA molecules contain all the instructions for the cell, and they're important in cell division.

2) If your cells are exposed to ionising radiation, the damage to DNA molecules can cause mutations, and the cells might start dividing over and over again, without stopping — this is cancer.

3) Very high doses of radiation can kill your cells altogether — this is what happens in 'radiation sickness'.

4) We're all exposed to ultraviolet radiation from the Sun. UV radiation is ionising, and can damage living cells in the skin. This can lead to sun burn or even skin cancer.

You Need Protection Against Dangerous Radiation

1) You can easily protect yourself from UV radiation from the Sun with physical barriers such as clothes or sunscreen/sunblock.

2) The ozone layer in the atmosphere (see p.63) also protects us (a bit) from UV radiation.

3) When you have an X-ray taken, the radiographer might put lead shields over parts of your body that aren't being investigated. The lead absorbs X-rays, protecting you from unnecessary exposure. Radiographers also wear lead aprons to protect themselves.

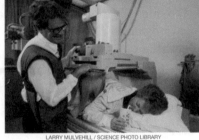

LARRY MULVEHILL / SCIENCE PHOTO LIBRARY

Use protection — wear a hat...

There's no point being paranoid about the dangers of radiation. Being exposed to high doses of X-rays doesn't mean you'll definitely get cancer — it increases the risk, but it's well worth having an X-ray to find out if you're seriously injured or ill. Sunbathing for hours with no protection is just stupid, though.

Some Uses of EM Radiation

No phones, no dinner — what would we do without EM radiation?

EM Radiation Can Cause Heating

1) Non-ionising radiation, e.g. light, doesn't have enough energy to break atoms up. When it's absorbed by a substance it transfers energy to the atoms or molecules of the substance — and heats them up.

2) The more intense the radiation (see p.59) and the longer the exposure, the greater the heating effect.

3) This heating effect can damage living cells, e.g. you get burned if you absorb too much infrared radiation.

4) Heating can be pretty useful though — it's how we cook food, after all. 'Normal' ovens do this with infrared radiation and microwave ovens do it with microwaves (surprise):

Microwaves heat up anything which contains particles that the microwaves can make vibrate. Some microwaves can heat water molecules. This is handy, because there's water in all food substances.

Microwave ovens come in different power ratings (e.g. 800 W, 1200 W). More powerful ovens produce higher intensity radiation, so less time is needed to produce the same heating effect — food cooks more quickly.

Microwave radiation would heat up the water in your body's cells if you were exposed to them. Microwave ovens have metal cases and screens over their glass doors which stop the microwaves getting out.

EM Radiation Can Transmit Information

EM radiation has been used to send information for years — e.g. using light to send signals in Morse code. There are quite a few more modern uses as well:

Infrared	TV remote controls 'Night vision' cameras
Microwave	Mobile phones, Satellite communication
Radio	TV and Radio transmissions Radar

Some People Say There Are Health Risks With Using Microwaves

1) When you make a call on your mobile, the phone emits microwave radiation. Some of this radiation is absorbed by your body, and causes heating of your body tissues (which all contain water).

2) There are concerns that heating of tissues like the brain and jaw, could increase the risk of some medical conditions, possibly including cancers. There is no conclusive evidence to show this, though.

3) The radiation is quite low intensity, so the heating is probably very minor and nothing to be too worried about. If you only talk for a short time, you'll minimise the effect (see above).

4) Mobile phone masts also emit microwave radiation. Some people who live very close to masts are worried about their possible effects. Again, there isn't much evidence — and any health problems might take a long time to emerge, so we might not know either way for many years.

Microwaves — for when you're only slightly sad to say goodbye...

Ovens and mobile phone networks both use microwaves, but with different energies. In an oven, the whole idea is for water molecules to absorb the microwave energy. But that's not ideal with a phone network — if the energy were absorbed by water molecules, the signals would never get through clouds.

EM Radiation and Life

No sunlight = no life. (Apart from a few very odd things right at the bottom of the sea, that is.)

Some Radiation from The Sun Passes Through The Atmosphere

1) The Earth is surrounded by an atmosphere made up of various gases — the air.

2) As you go further from the Earth's surface, the air gets thinner. (Mountaineers need to breathe oxygen from cylinders at very high altitudes because there isn't enough oxygen in the air to keep them alive.)

3) The gases in the atmosphere filter out certain types of radiation from the Sun — they absorb or reflect the radiation, so it never reaches the Earth's surface.

4) However, some types of radiation — mainly visible light and some radio waves — pass through the atmosphere quite easily.

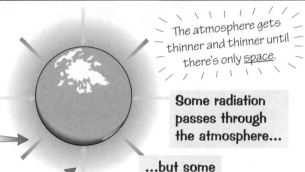

The atmosphere gets thinner and thinner until there's only space.

Some radiation passes through the atmosphere...

...but some doesn't.

Radiation Makes Photosynthesis (and Most Life) Possible

Almost all life on Earth depends on EM radiation from the Sun reaching us. This radiation does two jobs:

1) It helps keep the planet warm — during the day, the Earth's surface absorbs radiation and warms up.

2) Sunlight provides the energy for photosynthesis (the process by which green plants make their food — see below).

3) So, without the Sun, the planet would be too cold for life as we know it. There'd be also be no photosynthesis — so plants wouldn't grow, so animals couldn't feed on plants, so there'd be nothing to eat for anyone.

Photosynthesis Adds Oxygen to the Atmosphere

Photosynthesis is the process by which green plants make their food. This is what happens:

1) The plant takes in water from the soil and carbon dioxide from the air.

2) The plant's leaves (and other green parts, like the stem) absorb sunlight — so the energy of the light is transferred to the plant.

3) This energy is used in a chemical reaction between the water and the carbon dioxide.

4) The products of the reaction are sugar and oxygen. (Sugar is the plant's source of food.)

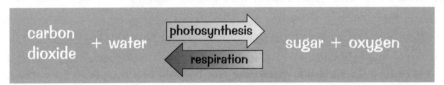

carbon dioxide + water → photosynthesis → sugar + oxygen
← respiration ←

5) So when plants photosynthesise, they remove carbon dioxide from the atmosphere and add oxygen.

6) This is the reverse of respiration (a reaction between glucose and oxygen which releases carbon dioxide and water into the atmosphere).

Let there be light...

The Sun emits all types of radiation, from radio to gamma rays. Most of the photons emitted in our direction never reach us though — they're absorbed by the atmosphere. The amount of light reaching us varies depending on how cloudy it is, but there's always enough to keep photosynthesis ticking over.

Module P2 — Radiation and Life

EM Radiation and The Atmosphere

The atmosphere <u>keeps us warm</u> by <u>trapping heat</u>.

The Greenhouse Effect Helps Regulate Earth's Temperature

1) The Earth <u>absorbs EM radiation</u> from the Sun (see previous page). This warms the Earth's surface up. The Earth then <u>emits</u> some of this EM radiation back out into space — this tends to cools us down.

2) Most of the radiation <u>emitted</u> from Earth is <u>infrared radiation</u> — <u>heat</u>.

3) A lot of this infrared radiation is <u>absorbed</u> by atmospheric gases, including <u>carbon dioxide</u>, <u>methane</u> and <u>water vapour</u>.

4) These gases then re-radiate heat in all directions, including <u>back towards the Earth</u>.

5) So the atmosphere acts as an insulating layer, stopping the Earth losing all its heat at night.

6) This is known as the 'greenhouse effect'. (In a greenhouse, the sun shines in and the glass helps keep some of the heat in.) <u>Without</u> the <u>greenhouse gases</u> (CO_2, methane, water) in our atmosphere, the Earth would be <u>a lot colder</u> than it is.

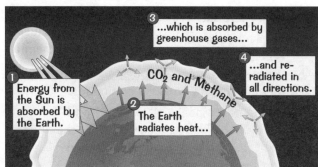

③ ...which is absorbed by greenhouse gases...

④ ...and re-radiated in all directions.

CO_2 and Methane

① Energy from the Sun is absorbed by the Earth.

② The Earth radiates heat...

The Ozone Layer Protects Us from Too Much UV Radiation

In part of the atmosphere, there's a gas called <u>ozone</u>.

1) Ozone is a form of <u>oxygen</u>. An ozone molecule is just <u>three oxygen atoms</u> joined together — O_3.

2) Ozone occurs naturally at a certain height in the atmosphere — the 'ozone layer'. It's formed like this:

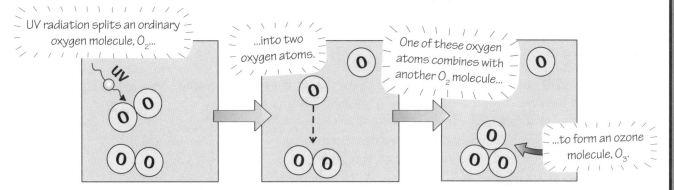

UV radiation splits an ordinary oxygen molecule, O_2...

...into two oxygen atoms.

One of these oxygen atoms combines with another O_2 molecule...

...to form an ozone molecule, O_3.

3) When an <u>ozone molecule</u>, O_3, absorbs more UV radiation, it splits into O_2 and O again. So the reaction can go forwards and backwards — it's a <u>reversible</u> chemical change.

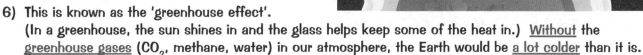

4) Without ozone, a lot more UV radiation (from the Sun) would reach us here on Earth.

5) UV is <u>ionising radiation</u> (see p.60) so it can be very harmful, especially to <u>complex</u> organisms (which have more complicated bits to go wrong) — this includes <u>humans</u> and many other <u>animals</u>.

6) So the <u>ozone layer</u> is very important — it <u>protects us</u> from too much UV radiation.

The ozone layer — free sunscreen...

We've been very careless with the ozone layer in the past, and made '<u>holes</u>' in it. We did this mainly by releasing gases called <u>CFCs</u> into the atmosphere. CFCs are man-made gases which used to be used in fridges and aerosols. They were phased out in the 1990s after we realised the damage they were doing.

The Carbon Cycle

Global warming and carbon emissions — you can't avoid hearing about them, so read on.

The Carbon Cycle Shows How Carbon is Naturally Recycled

Two of the 'greenhouse gases' which keep the Earth warm are carbon dioxide (CO_2) and methane (CH_4). There's a fairly small amount of CO_2 and just trace amounts (a tiny tiny bit) of methane. Both of these gases contain carbon.

1) All the carbon on Earth moves in a big cycle.

2) All plants and animals contain carbon. When they die, they start to decay — bacteria and fungi (decomposers) break them down into various compounds.

3) During decomposition, oxygen from the air combines with carbon from the plant, and carbon dioxide is released into the atmosphere. (This happens because the decomposers are respiring.)

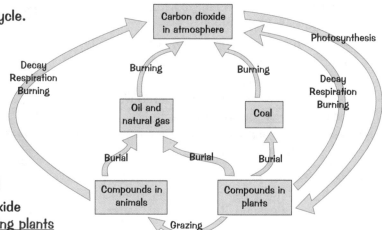

4) Other processes also release carbon dioxide into the air — including respiration in living plants and animals and burning (p.19).

5) Photosynthesis does the opposite — it removes carbon dioxide from the atmosphere (see p.62).

6) For thousands of years, these processes have all balanced out — and carbon dioxide has been removed from the air and added to the air in approximately equal quantities.

7) So the concentration of CO_2 in the atmosphere has been about the same for thousands of years. But recently that's been changing...

Humans Are Upsetting The Carbon Cycle

Over the last 200 years or so, the concentration of CO_2 in the atmosphere has been increasing. That must be because carbon dioxide is being released into the air faster than it's being removed. There are several reasons for this:

1) People's lifestyles have changed, e.g. we use more electrical gadgets, and travel more in cars and planes.

2) All this needs energy — which we get mainly from burning fossil fuels... which releases more carbon dioxide.

3) The population is rising, so more land is needed to build houses and grow food. This space is often made by chopping down and burning trees. This also adds to the carbon dioxide levels in the atmosphere:

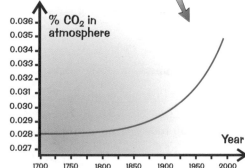

• Plants are the main things which remove carbon dioxide from the atmosphere (as they photosynthesise) — so fewer trees means less carbon dioxide is taken out of the atmosphere.

• Burning the trees adds lots of carbon dioxide into the atmosphere.

Eeeek — the carbon cycle's got a puncture...

For each person on a one-way flight from London to New York, a whopping 600 kg of carbon dioxide is added to the air. You can now pay to plant some trees to try and 'soak up' the carbon emissions you're responsible for. This sounds great, but there can be problems, e.g. for people living where the new plantations are planned. It might be better to release less CO_2 from fossil fuels in the first place.

Climate Change

Without any 'greenhouse gases' in the atmosphere, the Earth would be about 30 °C colder than it is now. So we <u>need</u> the greenhouse effect — just <u>not too much</u> of it...

Upsetting *the Greenhouse Effect Could Lead to* Climate Change

1) Since we started burning fossil fuels in a big way, levels of <u>carbon dioxide</u> in the atmosphere have risen (see previous page). The 'greenhouse' is now working too well and we're starting to <u>overheat</u>.

2) There's a lot of evidence to show that <u>global temperatures</u> have <u>risen</u> over the last century or so — and even a <u>small temperature rise</u> could have a <u>big effect</u> on the world's <u>climate</u>.

The *Consequences* of *Global Warming Could be Pretty Serious*

1) As the sea gets warmer, it will <u>expand</u>, causing sea levels to <u>rise</u>. This would be bad news for people living in low-lying places, like the Netherlands, East Anglia and the Maldives — they'd be flooded.

2) Higher temperatures make <u>ice melt</u>. Water that's currently 'trapped' on land (as ice) will run into the sea, causing sea levels to rise even more.

3) Weather patterns are likely to change in many parts of the world. It's thought that many regions will suffer more <u>extreme</u> weather, e.g. longer, hotter droughts. <u>Hurricanes</u> form over water that's warmer than 26 °C — so with more warm water, you'd expect <u>more hurricanes</u>.

4) These kinds of changes will affect <u>food production</u> — some regions would become <u>too dry</u> to grow food, some <u>too wet</u>.

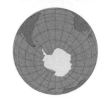

There's a lot of ice at the poles now, but is it melting?

Scientists Use *Computer Models to Predict* Climate Change

The climate is very complicated — conditions in the <u>atmosphere</u>, <u>oceans</u> and <u>land</u> all affect one another.

1) A <u>climate model</u> is a great big load of <u>equations</u> linking these various parts of the climate system. The idea is to mimic what goes on in the real climate by doing <u>calculations</u>.

HANK MORGAN / SCIENCE PHOTO LIBRARY

2) Once you've programmed a big <u>computer</u> with your equations, you need some <u>data</u> to start the calculations off. E.g. you might put in some data about <u>temperature</u> at the surface of the ocean in various places. The computer uses this data to work out, say, the speed and direction of ocean <u>currents</u>... then uses those results to work out <u>air temperatures</u> around the world. (It's a lot more complicated than this, but you don't have to know any details.)

3) Climate models are useful because you can 'play about' to see the effects of <u>changing various factors</u>. E.g. you could start with <u>more carbon dioxide</u> in the atmosphere and see how this would alter the climate in, say, 50 years' time. This is how scientists make <u>predictions</u> about <u>climate change</u>.

4) Climate models can be used to try and explain why the climate is changing <u>now</u>. We know that the Earth's climate <u>varies naturally</u> — changes in our orbit round the Sun cause ice ages, for instance. Most climate models show that <u>natural changes</u> <u>don't explain</u> the current 'global warming' — and that the increase in greenhouse gases caused by human activity is probably the main cause.

Be a climate model — go on a diet and solve lots of equations...

'Global warming' could mean that some parts of the world cool down. For instance, as ice melts, lots of cold fresh water will enter the sea and this could disrupt the <u>ocean currents</u>. This would be bad news for us in Britain — if the nice <u>warm</u> currents we get at the moment weaken, we'll be a lot colder.

Risks from EM Radiation

There are some risks that an individual person can't do much about — like climate change, for example. With other dangers, like harmful UV radiation from the Sun, you can minimise the risks quite easily.

Human Activities are Causing Global Warming

1) There is a correlation (link) between the concentration of CO_2 in the atmosphere and global temperature. When CO_2 levels are higher, temperatures are also higher.

2) Over the last 150 years or so, global temperatures have been rising ('global warming') and CO_2 levels have also been rising. This doesn't prove that rising CO_2 levels are causing global warming — it could be the other way round, or the two could be linked by a third variable (see p.3). However...

3) There's a plausible mechanism (a sensible explanation) of how rising CO_2 concentration could lead to rising temperatures — extra CO_2 acts like an extra 'blanket' around the Earth, trapping heat in the atmosphere. So it seems reasonable to say that rising CO_2 levels are causing global warming.

Ignoring Global Warming Could be Very Risky

1) Global warming could have some nasty consequences (see previous page). But there's a lot of uncertainty about what's most likely to happen and when and how serious the consequences would be.

2) Many people say we should adopt the 'precautionary principle' (see p.4) — assume that climate change will lead to serious havoc pretty soon, and act now to minimise the risk of this happening. This would mean cutting our carbon dioxide emissions — burning less fossil fuel, etc.

Sunbathing is a Risky Business Too

1) There's strong evidence to show that prolonged exposure to UV radiation (in sunlight) causes skin cancer.

2) This doesn't mean that everyone who spends a certain amount of time in the sun will get skin cancer. Your chances of developing skin cancer depend on many different factors — e.g. skin type, how often you got sunburnt as a child, use of sunscreen. We know this from various studies:

> E.g. A scientist might want to see whether people with very freckly skin are at higher risk of skin cancer. The study would have to compare the rates of skin cancer in two groups — people with lots of freckles and people with only a few freckles. The study would have to be designed carefully.
>
> 1) The samples have to be big enough — several thousand people rather than ten or twenty.
> 2) The sample groups must be well matched so that other factors don't influence the results. E.g. older people are more likely to develop skin cancer — so both samples should have the same number of people in each age group.

3) Using the ALARA principle (see p.4), people would minimise their exposure to UV radiation, e.g. by wearing sunscreen/sunblock, or by staying in the shade.

4) But some people sunbathe for hours on end, without using sunscreen — even though they know it increases their chances of getting cancer. It seems they're prepared to take the risk. That might be because they feel there are benefits (like getting a fashionable tan) which outweigh the risks. Or they might think the risk they're taking is lower than it really is.

Life — it's a risky business...

Finding correlations is an important part of many scientists' work. Remember, one piece of evidence isn't enough to show a link. For instance, noticing that 'I had cornflakes for breakfast' and 'I was late to school today' doesn't mean there's a correlation between cornflake-eating and lateness to school.

Revision Summary for Module P2

So, electromagnetic radiation — it's a bit weird, but if you can answer all these questions you're well on the way to a happy and fulfilled relationship with module P2.

1) What does radiation transfer?
2) Write out the electromagnetic spectrum, starting with radio waves on the left.
3) What is a photon?
4) Which has more energy — an infrared photon or an ultraviolet photon?
5) Name three sources of electromagnetic radiation.
6) State three things that might happen to radiation when it meets some matter.
7) When radiation is absorbed, what happens to its energy?
8) What does intensity mean?
9) Explain why the intensity of radiation decreases with distance from the source.
10) What is ionisation?
11) Name the three types of electromagnetic radiation which can cause ionisation.
12) Describe how ionising radiation can damage living cells.
13) Explain why excessive sunbathing can increase the risk of skin cancer.
14) Outline the measures people can take to minimise their exposure to radiation from:
   a) the Sun, b) hospital X-rays.
15) Explain why microwaves aren't ionising.
16) What effect does non-ionising radiation have on a substance that absorbs it?
17) Non-ionising radiation can damage living cells. Explain how.
18) Explain how a microwave oven cooks food.
19) Why are microwave ovens lined with metal?
20) Apart from microwave ovens, give another use of microwaves.
21) State two uses of: a) infrared radiation, b) radio waves.
22)*Some people think that using a mobile phone for long periods of time might pose a health risk. Explain why.
23) The Earth's atmosphere stops a lot of radiation reaching the surface of the planet. Describe how this happens.
24) Why is radiation from the Sun so important for life on Earth?
25) Outline the process of photosynthesis.
26) What are the products of respiration?
27) Name three 'greenhouse gases'.
28) Explain why we need some greenhouse gases in the atmosphere.
29) What is ozone?
30) Explain why the ozone layer is important for life on Earth.
31) Name two processes which add carbon dioxide to the atmosphere.
32) Suggest two reasons why there is more carbon dioxide in the atmosphere now than 200 years ago.
33) Explain how higher levels of carbon dioxide in the atmosphere are thought to lead to global warming.
34) How do scientists predict climate change?
35) Explain why global warming is expected to cause a rise in sea levels.
36) Why might rising sea levels be a problem?
37) Describe two other major problems that might be caused by climate change.
38)*What is a 'plausible mechanism'?

* Answers on page 104.

Evolution

Apologies if you don't believe in evolution, but it has to be learnt — think of it as just another theory.

Life on Earth is Incredibly Varied

1) There's an enormous number of species on Earth.

2) Scientists don't know how many species there are —
   estimates vary from 2 million to 100 million.

3) There are also loads of species that have become extinct so, since life
   began, a huge number of different living things have existed on the planet.

4) The very first living things were very simple. Life then
   evolved to become more complex and varied.

Algae are good examples of early, simple life forms.

5) All living things that exist now, and have ever existed, evolved from those very simple early life forms.

There is Good Evidence for Evolution

If you're going to say that living things evolved from very simple life forms, you need
to find good evidence for it. Fossil records and DNA both provide evidence for evolution:

> There is evidence for evolution in the fossil record, which shows
> species getting more and more complex as time goes on.

> DNA controls the characteristics of living things. It also
> mutates and changes over time. All living things have
> some similarities in their DNA, as you would expect if
> they have all evolved from the same simple life forms.
>
> The more closely related two species are, the more
> similar their DNA is. Scientists can use the similarities
> and differences in DNA to work out how life has evolved.

man

chimp

Humans and chimpanzees are closely related,
and about 95% of their DNA is the same.

Somehow, a Long Time Ago, Life Must Have Started

Scientists estimate that life on Earth began about 3500 million years ago.
There are three main ideas about how life first appeared:

① Many different religious groups believe that life was created by a god. The existence of
    God cannot be proved or disproved, and so this explanation is nothing to do with science.

② Some people believe that life arrived on Earth from outer space, possibly inside a meteorite.

③ Most scientists believe that life began when a chemical was formed that could copy itself and
    so 'reproduce'. Exactly how this could have happened is still uncertain. Experiments have
    shown that if you expose a mixture of the chemicals that were around on ancient Earth (water,
    ammonia, methane and hydrogen) to an electrical charge (like lightning), amino acids can
    form. Amino acids are the building blocks of proteins, which are the main constituent of cells.

It's life, Jim, but it's a bit hairy for my liking...

If you know the man in the picture, don't point and laugh at him. I thought it was funny to label him
'chimp', but, well, he might not find it all that funny himself. There were loads of famous people I
fancied putting in the book and labelling 'chimp', but sadly I'm not allowed to for legal reasons... Hmmf.

Natural Selection

This is important — read it carefully. If you don't understand <u>natural selection</u>, you won't get <u>evolution</u>.

Natural Selection Means the "Survival of the Fittest"

<u>Natural selection</u> is the <u>process</u> that causes <u>evolution</u>. It works like this:

1) Living things show <u>variation</u> — they are <u>not</u> all the same. OK, it's fairly simple so far.

2) The <u>resources</u> living things need to survive are limited. Individuals must compete for these resources to survive — only some of the individuals will survive.

3) Some of the <u>varieties</u> of a particular species will have a <u>better chance</u> of survival.
   Those varieties will then have an increased chance of <u>breeding</u> and passing on their <u>genes</u>.

4) This means that a <u>greater</u> proportion of individuals in the next generation will have the better <u>alleles</u>, and so the <u>characteristics</u>, that help <u>survival</u>.

5) Over many generations, the species becomes better and better able to <u>survive</u>. The 'best' features are <u>naturally selected</u> and the species becomes more and more <u>adapted</u> to its environment.

HERE'S AN EXAMPLE

Once upon a time maybe all rabbits had <u>short ears</u> and managed OK. Then one day out popped a rabbit with <u>big ears</u> who could hear better and was always the first to dive for cover at the sound of a predator. Pretty soon he's fathered a whole family of rabbits with <u>big ears</u>, all diving for cover before the other rabbits, and before you know it there are only <u>big-eared</u> rabbits left — because the rest just didn't hear trouble coming quick enough.

This is how populations <u>adapt</u> to survive better in their environment (an organism doesn't actually change when it's alive — changes only occur from generation to generation).

Over many generations the <u>characteristic</u> that <u>increased survival</u> becomes <u>more common</u> in the population. If members of a species are separated somehow, and evolve in different ways to adapt to different conditions, then over time you can end up with two totally <u>different species</u>.

The Best Genes for a Particular Environment Tend to Survive

The individuals who are <u>less suited</u> to an environment are <u>less likely</u> to survive than those that are better suited, and so have <u>less chance</u> to pass their <u>alleles</u> on. Gradually, over time, this results in a population which is extremely <u>well suited</u> to the environment in which it lives.

Remember — <u>variations</u> that are caused by the <u>environment</u> itself (e.g. accidentally losing a finger) <u>aren't</u> involved in natural selection. Variations in a species can have either <u>environmental</u> or <u>genetic causes</u>, but only the <u>genetic</u> ones are passed on to the next generation and influence the <u>evolution</u> of the species.

Artificial Selection is Where Humans Choose What Gets Selected

<u>Selective breeding</u> is sometimes called <u>artificial selection</u>. Selective breeding involves humans <u>deliberately choosing</u> a feature they want to appear in the next generation and only breeding from animals or plants that have it. Unlike natural selection, which only selects features that <u>help survival</u>, artificial selection may promote features that <u>don't</u> help survival.

> For example, a breeder might choose to only <u>breed</u> from the cows that produce the <u>most milk</u>, so that future generations of cows produce more milk than previous generations. This doesn't help the cow survive — instead it helps the farmer to make <u>money</u>.

"Natural Selection" — sounds like vegan chocolates...

It's no good being really great at surviving if for some reason you don't breed and <u>pass on your genes</u>. Also remember that it's only <u>genetic traits</u> that get passed on. So if you have funny ears, but have plastic surgery to make them nicer, your kids can still inherit your old ears, not your new prettier ones.

Producing New Species

Ooh, a page on producing <u>new species</u>. I'm going to make a species of humans with wings, armour-plating and spider-man style web-making equipment. Oh, this page doesn't tell you how to do that... Darn.

Mutations Happen When Genes Aren't Copied Properly

1) Over the course of life on Earth, many <u>new features</u> have appeared in animals and plants.

2) These have been caused by <u>'new' genes</u> that have been produced when existing genes <u>changed</u>.

3) These changes are called <u>mutations</u> — they happen all the time. Mutations can be caused by <u>outside factors</u> like <u>radiation</u> or <u>chemicals</u>, and by <u>mistakes</u> when genes are copied during cell division.

4) If mutations occur in <u>body cells</u>, they usually have little or <u>no effect</u>, though they can lead to cancer.

5) If they occur during the formation of <u>sex cells</u>, they have more effect, because the mutation will then be <u>passed on</u> to all the cells of the <u>offspring</u>. Such mutations can have one of these results:

- They may have <u>no effect</u> at all if they occur in an <u>unimportant</u> part of the DNA.
- They may cause an essential chemical to be <u>missing</u> or create a <u>new characteristic</u> that is <u>harmful</u>.
- <u>Sometimes</u>, they can produce a <u>new characteristic</u> that is of <u>benefit</u> to the species — an '<u>improvement</u>'.

Factors Can Combine to Create New Species

<u>New species</u> arise by a combination of different factors:

1) <u>Mutations</u> are necessary to create <u>new features</u>.

2) <u>Natural selection</u> works on the new features so that, if they are of <u>benefit</u>, they <u>spread</u> through a section of the population to create a <u>new species</u>.

3) <u>Environmental factors</u> also play a part. A new species is much more likely to form if a small population is '<u>cut off</u>' from others by some sort of <u>geographical barrier</u> (e.g. on an island).

Here's an <u>example</u> of how a new species could develop:

The snail species, <u>Cepaea nemoralis</u>, comes in two different colour varieties, <u>pink</u> and <u>yellow</u>. The data here shows their <u>distribution</u> in neighbouring areas of <u>woodland</u> and <u>grassland</u>.

- The <u>pink</u> snail is better camouflaged against the dead leaves in <u>woodland</u>.
- The <u>yellow</u> snail is better camouflaged in <u>grass</u>.

If the woodland and grassland were somehow <u>separated</u> so that the snail populations could not <u>inter-breed</u>, it is possible that two different 'species' would eventually develop — a pink species and a yellow species.

Numbers of pink and yellow snails found in two different habitats

No. snails (Woodland: Pink ~53, Yellow ~25; Grassland: Pink ~20, Yellow ~65)

- Pink snails
- Yellow snails

Life on Earth Could Easily Have Been Very Different

The <u>different species</u> that exist on Earth today are the result of the <u>changing conditions</u> that the planet has gone through. If some of the events in Earth's history had been <u>different</u>, then different types of organism would have been produced. For example:

The <u>dinosaurs</u> became <u>extinct</u> about 65 million years ago due to some sort of <u>environmental change</u> — a meteor impact, climate change or maybe a combination of factors. If this <u>hadn't</u> happened, the species that we'd see on Earth would be very different from the ones we have today.

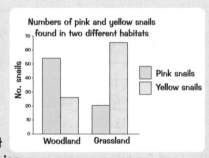

Crocophants and pandanzees — new species could be fun...

One thing you've got to remember is that new species developing is <u>very rare</u>. You're not likely to see a new species develop in your lifetime, for example. But <u>mutations</u> do happen and new species do develop sometimes. It all just happens very <u>slowly</u>, over thousands and thousands of years.

A Scientific Controversy

This page has got an <u>exciting</u> title — 'a scientific controversy' — ooh I love a bit of controversy I do.

Natural Selection Was a <u>Revolutionary Idea...</u>

<u>Charles Darwin</u> (1809–1882) was the first to propose the theory of <u>natural selection</u>. He came up with it through a combination of <u>imagination</u>, <u>opportunity</u> and <u>creativity</u>:

1) He had the <u>imagination</u> to see <u>beyond</u> the idea that all species are <u>unchangeable</u>, which is what nearly all scientists believed at the time.

2) His visit to the <u>Galapagos islands</u> put him in an area where there were lots of <u>islands</u>, close together yet <u>isolated</u> by the sea — <u>ideal conditions</u> for the evolution of <u>new species</u>.

3) Given this opportunity, he made careful <u>observations</u> and then applied a great deal of <u>analytical</u> and <u>creative thinking</u> to then come up with the idea of natural selection.

...Which <u>Upset</u> <u>Quite a Few People</u>

<u>Religious</u> people (i.e. most people at the time) <u>disliked</u> Darwin's ideas because his ideas disagreed with their belief that all species were created by <u>God</u>. However, that wasn't the only <u>reason</u> for his theory being rejected at first. There are <u>two</u> main reasons why scientists <u>disagreed</u> with Darwin at first:

(1) Natural selection is a <u>theory</u>. It is based on <u>interpretation</u> of observations and <u>ideas</u> which attempt to explain them. Different people can interpret things <u>differently</u> and there is always likely to be <u>disagreement</u> when there's no <u>absolute proof</u>.

(2) When new data <u>challenges</u> an accepted idea, you have to assume that <u>either</u> the <u>data</u> is wrong or the <u>original idea</u> is wrong. It would have been hard to change peoples' minds about where different species came from, so many would have automatically <u>assumed</u> that the <u>data</u> was wrong.

Not Everyone <u>Thinks the Theory of Natural Selection is</u> True

Many scientists are <u>convinced</u> that natural selection is the best explanation for evolution, but some <u>aren't sure</u>, and others (e.g. <u>creationists</u>) don't believe that <u>evolution</u> has happened at all. It's hard for some people to make their minds up about natural selection. Here's why:

1) The <u>data</u> may be <u>reliable</u>, but most reports only offer one <u>interpretation</u> of the data, when others may be possible. Scientists may also choose to <u>ignore</u> any data that <u>conflicts</u> with their own ideas.

2) Natural selection seems a <u>good</u> explanation for the way things <u>adapt</u> to their environment — it can explain how many features of animals and plants could have appeared. However, it's <u>not so good</u> at explaining the evolution of <u>complex features</u> like the eye, and the evolution of <u>unique</u> new species. (Opponents concentrate on these <u>weaker</u> areas to challenge the <u>whole</u> idea of natural selection.)

3) Ideas about exactly how natural selection works have <u>changed</u> over the years and are <u>still changing</u> as <u>new data</u> becomes available.

Not as controversial as I was expecting...

I feel a bit sorry for Darwin. He came up with such a great <u>theory</u>, but nobody believed him for ages. Apparently, he knew the reaction he'd get from the religious community, so he was planning on leaving the publication of his theory until after his death. It was <u>only</u> when some other scientist came up with a similar theory that Darwin thought it was time to get on and publish. And it all kicked off...

Human Evolution

Well I don't know if it's just me, but I think this section is really <u>interesting</u>. It's amazing to think that your super-distant relatives are <u>apes</u> — before that, we were squirrelly things, and before that, <u>fish</u>... Er, maybe.

The Big Human Brain Gave a Big Survival Advantage

We human beings have a <u>brain</u> that is very <u>large</u> in relation to the rest of our body, <u>compared</u> to other animals. The <u>evolution</u> of this larger brain gave ancient humans a big <u>advantage</u> when it came to <u>survival</u>:

1) It allowed them to <u>solve problems</u> better, and to develop effective <u>tools</u>. This would have been particularly useful in <u>hunting</u>, allowing them to capture more <u>food</u>.

2) The larger brain also allowed humans to develop ways of <u>communicating</u>, so that <u>ideas</u> could be shared. This would have been useful in group hunting.

The Human 'Family Tree' Shows Where We Came From

The diagram below shows the latest idea on how humans (<u>Homo sapiens</u>) <u>evolved</u>.

You don't need to remember all the details of the diagram, but the following basic principles are important:

1) There have been quite a lot of different species of human on the planet, and all except <u>Homo sapiens</u> (us) are now <u>extinct</u>.

2) All human species are thought to have evolved from a <u>common ancestor</u>, which lived about 5 million years ago.

3) <u>Hominids</u> (human-like species) have evolved in <u>different ways</u>, as shown by the <u>branching</u> in the diagram.

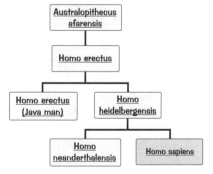

The Theory of Human Evolution Might be Wrong

The problem with working out how humans evolved is that all the other human species are <u>extinct</u>, and the only <u>evidence</u> we have about them is often just a few <u>bones</u>.

The <u>human family tree</u> has been worked out on the basis of <u>similarities</u> and <u>differences</u> between <u>bones</u> found in different places. This evidence matches the family tree, but it <u>doesn't</u> mean the tree is absolutely <u>correct</u>.

Here's an example which proves you <u>shouldn't believe</u> every piece of evidence found:

More evidence like this would be useful.

PILTDOWN MAN

In 1912, the discovery of <u>skull</u> and <u>jawbone</u> fragments seemed to provide evidence of a <u>missing link</u> between apes and humans. This evidence became known as '<u>Piltdown man</u>' after the English village where it was found. The jawbone was <u>ape-like</u>, but the skull was like that of a <u>modern man</u>. The evidence suggested that humans might have evolved in a <u>different</u> way from what was currently believed. However, 30 years later it was found to be a <u>forgery</u>. Shocking news.

Since Piltdown man was proved to be <u>fake</u>, many people have suggested that this <u>weakens</u> the <u>whole</u> theory of human evolution. However, since the Piltdown man evidence <u>didn't</u> fit in with the theory of human evolution anyway, it was the <u>observation</u> and not the <u>theory</u> that was proved to be incorrect.

I know some teachers who look like they need to evolve...

You don't need to remember all the details about Piltdown man. He's just there as an example to show you that if an observation seems to <u>change</u> an <u>existing</u> theory, then either the <u>observation</u> or the <u>theory</u> must be <u>wrong</u>. In this case, Piltdown man was a fake — I wonder who made him and why they did it.

The Nervous System

We were once really <u>simple</u> organisms, made of just a few cells, and now we have <u>eyes</u> and <u>lungs</u> and a massive great <u>brain</u> capable of so many exciting things. It makes you wonder at the power of nature.

Evolution Eventually Led to Some Very Complicated Organisms

As multicellular organisms got <u>bigger</u>, they got more <u>complicated</u>, developing different parts that were <u>specialised</u> for different jobs. Once that happened, they needed ways to <u>communicate</u> with and <u>coordinate</u> the different parts. To do this, animals evolved <u>nervous</u> and <u>hormonal</u> communication systems. The nervous system is for <u>fast</u>, <u>short-lived</u> responses like moving muscles.

The Nervous System Lets You React to Stimuli

A <u>stimulus</u> is a <u>change in your environment</u> which you may need to react to (e.g. a recently pounced tiger). You need to be constantly monitoring what's going on so you can respond if you need to.

1) You have five different <u>sense organs</u> — <u>eyes</u>, <u>ears</u>, <u>nose</u>, <u>tongue</u> and <u>skin</u>.

2) They all contain different <u>receptors</u>. Receptors are groups of cells which are <u>sensitive</u> to a <u>stimulus</u>. They change <u>stimulus energy</u> (e.g. light energy) into <u>electrical impulses</u>.

3) A stimulus can be <u>light</u>, <u>sound</u>, <u>touch</u>, <u>pressure</u>, <u>chemical</u>, or a change in <u>position</u> or <u>temperature</u>.

> <u>Sense organs</u> and <u>receptors</u>
> Don't get them mixed up:
>
> The <u>eye</u> is a <u>sense organ</u> — it contains <u>light receptors</u>.
>
> The <u>ear</u> is a <u>sense organ</u> — it contains <u>sound receptors</u>.

The <u>five sense organs</u> and the <u>receptors</u> that each contains are:

1) <u>Eyes</u>   <u>Light</u> receptors.

2) <u>Ears</u>   <u>Sound</u> and "<u>balance</u>" receptors.

3) <u>Nose</u>   <u>Smell</u> receptors — sensitive to chemical stimuli.

4) <u>Tongue</u>   <u>Taste</u> receptors: — sensitive to bitter, salt, sweet and sour, plus the taste of savoury things like monosodium glutamate (MSG) — chemical stimuli.

5) <u>Skin</u>   Sensitive to <u>touch</u>, <u>pressure</u> and <u>temperature change</u>.

<u>Sensory Neurones</u>
The <u>nerve cells</u> that carry signals as <u>electrical impulses</u> from the <u>receptors</u> in the sense organs to the <u>central nervous system</u>.

<u>Motor Neurones</u>
The <u>nerve cells</u> that carry signals from the CNS to the <u>effector</u> muscles or glands.

The Central Nervous System Coordinates a Response

1) <u>The central nervous system</u> (CNS) is where all the information from the sense organs is <u>sent</u>, and where reflexes and actions are <u>coordinated</u>.

   The central nervous system consists of <u>the brain</u> and <u>spinal cord</u> only.

2) <u>Neurones</u> (nerve cells) <u>transmit the information</u> (as <u>electrical impulses</u>) very quickly to and from the CNS.

3) "<u>Instructions</u>" from the CNS are sent to the <u>effectors</u> (<u>muscles and glands</u>), which respond accordingly.

<u>Effectors</u>
Muscles and glands are known as <u>effectors</u> — they respond in different ways.
<u>Muscles contract</u> in response to a nervous impulse, whereas <u>glands secrete hormones</u>.

Hormones

OK, so this page is called 'hormones', but there's some stuff about nerves in it too. Just to warn you...

Hormones Are Chemical Messengers Sent in the Blood

1) Hormones are chemicals released directly into the blood. They are carried in the blood plasma to other parts of the body, but only affect particular cells (called target cells) in particular places.

2) Hormones control things in organs and cells that need constant adjustment.

3) They are produced in various glands, as shown here, and travel through your body at "the speed of blood".

4) Hormones tend to have relatively long-lasting effects (compared to nerves whose effects don't last long at all).

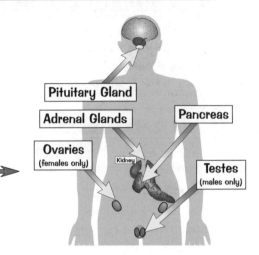

Pituitary Gland
Adrenal Glands
Pancreas
Ovaries (females only)
Kidney
Testes (males only)

Learn These Examples of Communication in your Body

Examples of nervous communication are:

1) Picking something up — your brain instructs the muscles of your arm, hand and fingers to move in the desired way.

2) Vision — your eyes detect patterns of light and then send a signal to the brain, which builds up the picture of what you are seeing.

Examples of hormonal communication are:

1) When you are scared or angry, your adrenal glands produce the hormone adrenaline. This gives you more energy to respond as it increases your breathing and heart rate, and directs blood to your muscles.

2) When your blood sugar rises after a meal, the pancreas releases the hormone insulin. This acts all over your body to help you use up or store the sugar.

Homeostasis Involves Nerves and Hormones

In order to keep a constant internal environment ('homeostasis'), several different organs need to communicate with each other. This involves both the nervous and hormonal communication systems.

1) Temperature control depends on the body's ability to detect temperature. This is done by the nervous system. Most of the responses which regulate our body temperature (e.g. shivering, hair standing on end) are also under nervous control.

2) Water levels and blood sugar levels are mostly controlled by hormones. Hormones control the function of the kidneys to keep water level under control, and blood sugar is controlled by hormones produced by the pancreas.

Learn about homeostasis — and keep your cool...

'Homeostasis' is an important word — it means maintaining the right conditions inside your body so that everything works properly. So that means removing waste products if they build up, keeping ions, water and sugar at the right levels, and keeping your temperature right — not too hot and not too cold.

Interdependence

As a slight detour from nerves and hormones, here's some stuff on interdependence.
Interdependence is about how nearly all species are dependent on a number of other species for survival.

Every Living Thing Needs Resources from its Environment

The environment in which an organism lives provides it with factors that are essential for life. These include:

1) Light (needed by plants to make food)
2) Food (for animals) and minerals (for plants)
3) Oxygen (for animals and plants) and carbon dioxide (for plants)
4) Water (vital for all living organisms)

If any essential factor in a habitat is in short supply, the different species that need it have to compete for it. If there's not enough to go around, some organisms won't survive. This will limit the size of their populations in that habitat.

Any Change in Any Environment can Have Knock-on Effects...

The interdependence of all the living things in a habitat means that any major change in the habitat can have far-reaching effects.

The diagram on the right shows part of a food web from a stream.

Stonefly larvae are particularly sensitive to pollution. Suppose pollution killed them in this stream. The table below shows some of the effects this might have on some of the other organisms in the food web.

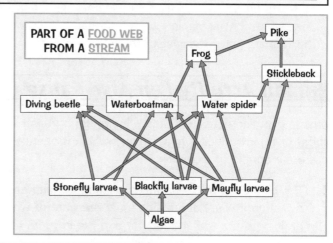

PART OF A FOOD WEB FROM A STREAM

Organism	Effect of loss of stonefly larvae	Effect on population
Blackfly larvae	Less competition for algae	Increase
	More likely to be eaten by predators	Decrease
Water spider	Less food	Decrease
Stickleback	Less food (if water spider or mayfly larvae numbers decrease)	Decrease

Remember that food webs are very complex and that these effects are difficult to predict accurately.

...Even Possibly Extinction

The fossil record contains many species that don't exist any more — these species are said to be extinct. Dinosaurs and mammoths are extinct animals, with only fossils to tell us they existed at all.

Rapid change in the environment can cause a species to become extinct. Here are three changes that could cause extinction:

1) The environmental conditions change (e.g. destruction of habitat).
2) A new species is introduced which is a competitor, disease organism or predator of that species (this could include humans hunting them).
3) An organism in its food web that it is reliant on becomes extinct.

I'm dependent on the coffee plant...

If you're asked to analyse the consequences of a change in a food web, consider 'knock-on' effects as well as the organisms which are directly affected. You'll find that there are loads of different possible things that could happen — so just be aware of all the possibilities and you'll be sure of good marks.

Humans and the Earth

This page is about how we've caused <u>extinction</u> in the past, either <u>directly</u> by just blatantly killing things, or <u>indirectly</u> by doing other irresponsible things. It's also on why making species extinct is a <u>bad</u> idea.

Human Activity **Can Directly** Cause Extinction

Many organisms have become <u>extinct</u> in the past, and many are <u>threatened</u> with extinction now. A lot of extinction is due to <u>human activities</u>. In some cases, humans have caused extinction <u>directly</u>. For example:

1) The <u>dodo</u> was a large flightless bird discovered in Mauritius when Portuguese sailors landed there in 1598. It was easy to <u>hunt</u> because it couldn't fly, and within 100 years it was <u>extinct</u>.

GEORGE BERNARD / SCIENCE PHOTO LIBRARY

2) The '<u>Tasmanian wolf</u>' was hunted to extinction on the island of Tasmania in the early 20th century. Humans first reduced its numbers by destroying its <u>habitat</u> to set up sheep <u>farms</u>. Then when the Tasmanian wolves started eating the sheep, the farmers <u>killed</u> the rest of them.

Human Activity **Can Also** Cause Extinction **Indirectly**

Humans can also cause extinction <u>indirectly</u> by destroying an organism's <u>habitat</u> or by introducing <u>new species</u> which it cannot compete with. Here are a couple of examples:

(1) The <u>blue pike</u> from the Great Lakes in Canada became extinct in 1970. Although it was hunted, the main reasons for extinction were the <u>draining</u> of its wetland habitat and the introduction of <u>new species</u> which reduced blue pike numbers due to predation and competition.

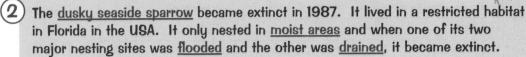

(2) The <u>dusky seaside sparrow</u> became extinct in 1987. It lived in a restricted habitat in Florida in the USA. It only nested in <u>moist areas</u> and when one of its two major nesting sites was <u>flooded</u> and the other was <u>drained</u>, it became extinct.

Earth's Biodiversity **is Important**

Having a <u>variety</u> of animals and plants on Earth is called <u>biodiversity</u>. <u>Maintaining</u> biodiversity, rather than causing species to become extinct, is an important part of using the environment in a <u>sustainable</u> way. Here are three reasons why:

1) Every living organism plays a <u>role</u> in its ecosystem. Research suggests that biodiversity makes ecosystems more <u>stable</u> and more able to <u>resist</u> and <u>recover</u> from damage.

2) The more <u>plants</u> we have available, the more <u>resources</u> there are for developing <u>new food crops</u>.

3) Many new <u>medicines</u> have been discovered using chemicals produced by living things. For example, <u>digitalis</u>, a drug used to treat heart disease, was discovered in the <u>foxglove</u>. When a living organism becomes <u>extinct</u>, the unique chemicals it produces are no longer available.

Dodo in batter please...

I'm sure you already knew that letting things become extinct isn't good. What you probably didn't know, though, is how it's often the fault of us <u>humans</u> that these species are gone for good. We now need to make sure we don't let anything else become extinct — we must think about <u>sustainable development</u>.

Revision Summary for Module B3

Well, I know I'm biased, but I thought that was a thoroughly interesting section. Evolution is quite amazing really, and always sparks a good few debates. I personally love bringing it up at parties — asking whether people knew that they had monkeys for relatives always stirs up a bit of conflict. Anyway, you know what time it is now. It's question time...

1)   How many different species are there? A few? Hundreds? Thousands? Or millions?

2)   How do fossils provide evidence that we evolved from simpler life forms?

3)   How do scientists use DNA evidence to back up the theory of evolution?

4)   What are the three main ideas of how life first appeared on Earth?

5)   True or false — If an organism randomly develops a feature that gives it a survival advantage, then it will be more likely to survive than other organisms, and will also be more likely to produce offspring which also have this advantageous feature. Eventually, many organisms will have the feature.

6)* Imagine a person was born with super-human features like X-ray vision and bullet-proof skin (which offer a massive survival advantage), but they had no desire to seek out members of the opposite sex to make babies. Would these super-human features end up being 'naturally selected'?

7)   Give an example of a feature that has been artificially selected by humans in farm animals or crops.

8)   When lambs have their tails removed, do their future offspring end up with tails or no tails?

9)   Which has a greater effect on a species — mutations in body cells or mutations in sex cells?

10) List the three main things that could happen as the result of a mutation in a sex cell.

11)* How might a geographical barrier help to create a new species?

12) True or false — If the dinosaurs hadn't been killed off, we'd have different species on Earth today.

13) Why didn't some religious people agree with Darwin's theory of natural selection?

14) What non-religious reasons are there for people not believing Darwin's theory of natural selection?

15) Why was evolving a big brain a survival advantage for humans?

16) True or false — Human species other than *Homo sapiens* still exist today?

17) Who was Piltdown man? Did his evidence change the theory of human evolution?

18) List the five sense organs and say what receptors they contain.

19) What does CNS stand for? What does the CNS do?

20) Explain the difference between sensory and motor neurones.

21) How fast do hormones travel through your body?

22) Give one example of nervous communication and one example of hormonal communication.

23) What's that funny word that means 'maintaining a constant internal environment'?

24) List four factors that are essential for plants to live.

25) True or false — In a food web, if one organism dies out, the other organisms will be unaffected?

26) What are the three main reasons for a species becoming extinct?

27) Give an example of a species that humans directly wiped out. How did they do this?

28) Give an example of a species that humans wiped out indirectly. Explain what happened.

29)* Why should we not just run riot making every species extinct other than our own?

* Answers on page 104.

Recycling Elements

Thought recycling was a new idea developed by hippies in the 1970s? It turns out that clever old mother nature's been recycling stuff for millions of years. And she never wore tie-dye either.

Elements are Constantly Being Recycled

There isn't a never-ending supply of the elements that living things need, so they have to be recycled.

1) As plants grow they take in elements like oxygen, nitrogen and carbon through their leaves and roots. They're often in the form of compounds, e.g. as water and carbon dioxide.

2) When the plants die and decompose, most of these elements are returned to the soil. Others go into the air as gases like methane.

3) Some of the elements in plants become part of animals when the plants are eaten. These elements are also returned to the environment when the animals poo or when they die and decompose.

4) Dead animal and plant matter (and animal waste) is broken down by microbes. They convert it into compounds that are taken up by other plants and the whole process starts again.

The Nitrogen Cycle is a Good Example of Recycling an Element

The constant cycling of nitrogen through the atmosphere, soil and organisms is called the nitrogen cycle.

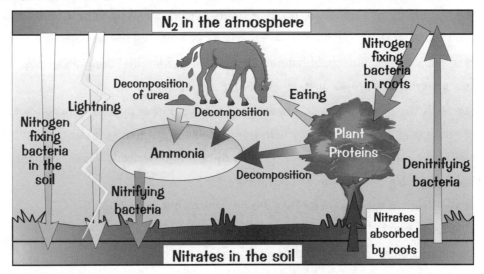

1) Plants absorb nitrogen in the form of nitrates from the soil. Nitrogen is needed by plants and animals so that they can make proteins (see p. 81).

2) Animals have to eat plants (or other animals) to get their nitrogen.

3) Any organic waste, i.e. rotting plants, dead animals and animal poo, is broken down by microbes called decomposers into ammonium compounds.

4) Nitrifying bacteria turn the ammonium compounds produced by the microbes into useful nitrates.

5) These nitrates can then be absorbed by the roots of green plants once again.

6) A couple of extra weird bits worth mentioning — nitrogen-fixing bacteria live in the soil and the roots of some plants and can cleverly make nitrates directly from nitrogen in the air. Energy from lightning can also make nitrogen and oxygen in the air react to give nitrates in the soil. But denitrifying bacteria do the opposite and break down nitrates in the soil to give nitrogen in the air again.

It's the cyyyycle of liiiiife...

I guess it's pretty obvious really — there's only so much stuff on Earth and so it has to be recycled. Make sure you understand the basic principles at the top of the page and the details of the nitrogen cycle. By the way, there are about a million different ways of drawing the nitrogen cycle, so don't be put off if there's one in the exam that looks a bit different to this one — the basic ideas are the same.

Organic and Intensive Farming

Thought farming was all much of a muchness? Well think again, because there are two distinctly different ways of producing food — organic farming and intensive farming.

Harvesting Crops Removes Elements from the Soil

All crops are eventually harvested and removed from the field so that they can be sold and eaten.

1) The removal of the crops means that some of the elements that the plants used to grow are taken out of the field for good, instead of being returned to the soil when the plants die and decay.

2) Elements that are lost include nitrogen, phosphorus and potassium.

3) These elements need to be replaced or the fertility of the soil will decrease and the next crop of plants won't grow properly.

4) The way that farmers replace the lost elements depends on whether they farm organically or intensively.

Different Farming Methods Replace Lost Elements Differently

① Organic Farming Relies on the Natural Recycling of Organic Matter

Artificial fertilisers are banned in organic farming, so natural substances and processes are used instead.

1) Organic farmers put animal manure, compost and human sewage onto their land as fertilisers. The human sewage is heat-treated first to destroy harmful microbes.

2) Manure, sewage and compost all contain waste plant material, so they replace the elements that plants take out of the soil in the same way as a natural cycle would (see p. 78).

3) Organic farmers also grow "green manure". Plants are grown on fields and then ploughed in and left to rot. Plants like clover are often used because they have nitrogen-fixing bacteria in their roots which add nitrates to the soil (see p. 78). The nitrates can then be used by the next crop.

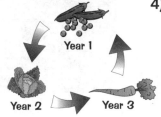

4) Organic farmers also use crop rotation to help keep their soil fertile. They grow different crops each year in a cycle — for example, peas might be grown one year, cabbage the next and carrots in year three. The peas contain nitrogen-fixing bacteria like clover does, so they help prepare the soil for the cabbage crop, which particularly needs nitrates. Carrots don't need much nitrogen, so they can still grow in the soil after the cabbage crop. And then it's back to the peas again.

② Intensive Farming Relies on Artificial Fertilisers

1) Intensive farmers use man-made artificial fertilisers to put elements back into the soil.

2) Because artificial fertilisers are pure chemicals (i.e. they're not full of plant matter), it's easy to use just the right amount. Farmers can use small volumes of artificial fertilisers, because they contain much higher percentages of the elements the crops need than manure does.

3) Artificial fertilisers are spread on the ground as pellets or sprayed onto the crops as they grow.

4) The crops will grow better than an organic crop would, because the amount of each nutrient can be exactly right for a particular plant's needs. You can also grow whatever crop you want, year after year.

5) But covering plants in chemicals isn't exactly healthy, and if the fertiliser washes into nearby rivers it can cause environmental problems like eutrophication. This is where water plants grow really well, then die and are broken down by bacteria. The bacteria flourish and use up all the oxygen and the fish die.

So that's intensive farming — now do some intensive revision...

It's easy to paint intensive farming as the bad guy nowadays, but you can see why everyone was once so pleased with it. Big yields of good quality food at cheap prices — it was hard to see a disadvantage.

Organic and Intensive Farming

So you've got all the nutrients your crop needs in the soil and everything looks rosy (especially if you're growing roses). But just when you thought nothing could go wrong, bam... a plague of locusts. Oh no.

There are Different Ways to Deal With Pests and Disease

Pests and disease are an absolute nightmare for farmers because they can seriously reduce crop yields.

1) Some pests, like Colorado beetles and aphids, are insects that eat crop plants.

2) Diseases like potato blight and botrytis can damage or kill crop plants.

3) Some pests and diseases affect the way crops look, making them harder to sell.

Luckily, most pests and diseases can be controlled. The methods used depend on the type of farming.

1 Organic Farming Uses Natural Biological Processes

Organic farmers aren't allowed to use man-made chemicals to deal with pests and diseases.

1) Pests are controlled using natural predators — this is known as biological control. For example, ladybirds are introduced into greenhouses to prey on greenfly pests.

2) Crop rotation (see p. 79) is used to prevent the pests and diseases of one particular crop plant building up in an area.

3) Field edges are left grassy to encourage larger insects and other animals that feed on pests.

4) Varieties of plants that are best able to resist pests and diseases are chosen.

2 Intensive Farming Relies on Chemicals

Intensive farmers spray their crops with man-made chemicals to destroy pests and diseases.

1) Chemical pesticides are more effective than organic methods. They usually kill all of the pests and diseases that threaten the crops, which organic methods can't do.

2) This means a bigger yield of more attractive fruits or vegetables.

3) But it's not all good — the spraying leaves a chemical residue on the crop. This could harm humans eating the plants, as well as the pests.

4) Chemical pesticides don't just kill pests, but all kinds of harmless and beneficial animals too. This disrupts food chains and decreases biodiversity.

Organic Farmers Have to Follow Certain Rules

It's illegal to sell food as organic if it hasn't really been grown that way.

1) The UK government has set national standards that have to be met by organic farmers, e.g. concerning the use of chemicals. There are also other schemes, like the one set up by the Soil Association (an environmental charity), to make sure that food labelled 'organic' can be trusted.

2) The national rules ban the use of virtually all artificial chemicals and set standards for the way that pests and diseases are controlled. The levels of pesticides and other artificial chemicals in the soil have to be below a certain level before a farm can be classed as organic.

3) The standards for meat that is classed as organic are just as strict. The animals must be allowed to move around freely, can only be fed on organic feed and can't be given artificial hormones to make them grow more quickly. They're not given medication unless it's really necessary, unlike intensively reared animals, which are often given antibiotics as a matter of course because infections are so common.

I'm arresting you on suspicion of carrot fraud...

Both types of farming have their own costs and benefits — for the general public, the environment, the farmers, etc. Organic farming is more expensive and you can't grow as much in one area, but it is more sustainable as it's less harmful to the environment and you don't have to manufacture chemicals.

Natural Polymers

When you think about polymers (if you ever do), you probably think of the man-made kind, like plastics. But as usual mother nature got there first. And her polymers don't choke seagulls and stuff either.

Carbohydrates and Proteins are Natural Polymers

Many of the chemicals found naturally in living things are long-chain molecules called polymers. Polymers are large molecules formed by combining lots of smaller molecules (called monomers) in a regular pattern.

1) Complex carbohydrates are polymers built by linking together simple sugars like glucose. A complex carbohydrate called cellulose is the main structural material in all plants.

2) Proteins are huge polymer molecules built by linking small molecules called amino acids. There are about 20 natural amino acids that can be joined in different ways to make the thousands of different proteins found in living things (see p. 82 for examples).

Carbohydrates Consist of Carbon, Hydrogen and Oxygen

Carbohydrates are a group of compounds that include sugars (the monomers) and the polymers cellulose, starch and glycogen. They're all made up of the same elements — carbon, hydrogen and oxygen.

1) In carbohydrates the number of hydrogen atoms is always double the number of oxygen atoms (and it's the same in water). The name 'carbohydrate' comes from the fact that they're basically made of carbon and water.

2) The simplest carbohydrate is the sugar glucose, $C_6H_{12}O_6$. This is the sugar that plants make in their leaves, from carbon dioxide and water, by photosynthesis.

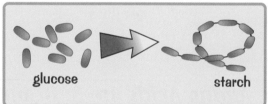
glucose   starch

3) Other sugars like glycogen (for energy storage in animals), starch (for energy storage in plants) and cellulose are made by linking glucose molecules together in chains.

Proteins Contain Carbon, Hydrogen, Oxygen and Nitrogen

Proteins are a huge group of compounds. They're all made from amino acids and consist mostly of carbon, hydrogen, oxygen and nitrogen.

1) Plants take in nitrates from the soil and react them with glucose from photosynthesis to make amino acids. The amino acids are then linked together to make the proteins the plant needs.

2) Animals get their amino acids from plants. They break down plant proteins during digestion to give amino acids, and then join them back up in a new order in their cells to make new proteins.

3) Amino acids all have the same basic structure with slight variations.

4) Amino acids link together into long chains — these are proteins.

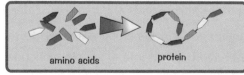
amino acids   protein

5) There are only about 20 different amino acids. It's the order in which they're connected up that makes each protein different.

Zzzzzzzzzzzzzzzz... What? Who? No, of course I wasn't asleep...

It's pretty mind-numbing this, isn't it? Still, dull pages are bound to crop up from time to time and you've just got to grit your teeth and learn them. If you're still awake please learn the elements that carbohydrates and proteins are made from — that's the key thing you need to know.

Digestion

You get <u>food</u> from animals and plants. But you don't want <u>their</u> carbohydrates and proteins, you want your own <u>human-type</u> ones. So first you <u>break down</u> the polymers you eat, and then you <u>build new ones</u>.

Digestion Involves Breaking Down Big Molecules

After you've chewed your food up and your stomach's had its turn at churning it up even further, it's still made up of <u>quite big molecules</u>, namely: <u>starch</u>, <u>proteins</u> and <u>fats</u>.

These are still <u>too big</u> to diffuse into the blood, and so they are broken down in the <u>small intestine</u> into <u>smaller</u>, <u>soluble</u> molecules like <u>glucose</u> and <u>amino acids</u>. These can then move into the <u>blood</u> and be transported to all the cells of the body where they're needed.

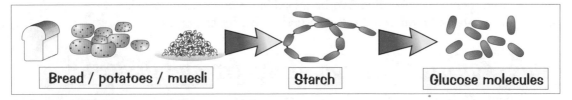

Bread / potatoes / muesli   Starch   Glucose molecules

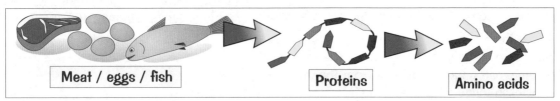

Meat / eggs / fish   Proteins   Amino acids

Amino Acids Are Built up into New Proteins

1) As cells <u>grow</u> they need new <u>proteins</u>, which they make from the <u>amino acids</u> flowing past in the blood. Each protein has a different <u>sequence</u> of amino acids, just as words use the same letters in different orders (see p. 81).

2) Most of your body is made from proteins. They're the main part of your <u>skin</u>, <u>hair</u>, <u>nails</u>, <u>muscles</u> and <u>tendons</u>. All the <u>enzymes</u> that control your body's <u>reactions</u> are proteins too.

3) <u>Haemoglobin</u>, the red substance in <u>red blood cells</u>, is a protein called <u>globin</u> attached to a substance called <u>haem</u>. Haem contains <u>iron</u> and is the substance that carries <u>oxygen</u> around your body.

Excess Amino Acids Are Disposed of in Urine

Animals often eat protein that contains <u>more</u> amino acids than they can use at once. The body <u>can't</u> usually store amino acids and use them later on, so they have to be <u>excreted</u> instead.

1) <u>Excess</u> amino acids in the blood are taken to the <u>liver</u> to be broken down.

2) They are converted first into <u>ammonia</u>, which is poisonous, and then into a soluble substance called <u>urea</u> which is safe to release into the blood.

3) As the blood passes through your <u>kidneys</u>, the dissolved urea is removed and passes out of the body in the <u>urine</u>. The average adult excretes about <u>30 g</u> of urea <u>every day</u>.

Digestion? I'm sure they told me this was chemistry...

Ah you see, it's not like the old days when <u>biology</u> was <u>pondweed</u>, <u>chemistry</u> was <u>Bunsen burners</u> and <u>physics</u> was <u>light bulbs</u>. Now that you're older, science is all overlapping and full of issues and arguing. It's more <u>relevant</u> to <u>real life</u>, of course — but sometimes I still kind of miss the Bunsen burners.

Insulin and Diabetes

Everyone knows that it's <u>not</u> healthy to eat loads of <u>processed foods</u> and to be <u>overweight</u>, and yet loads of us still eat junk. That's why more people are developing <u>type 2 diabetes</u>, and at a younger age too.

Diabetes is When The Body Can't Control Blood Sugar Levels

The body produces a hormone called <u>insulin</u> in the <u>pancreas</u>. Insulin helps the body convert <u>sugar</u> (glucose) in the blood into <u>energy</u>, or to <u>store</u> it. The amount of insulin you produce depends on your blood sugar level. The more sugar you've eaten and released into the blood, the more insulin is produced.

1) <u>Processed foods</u> often contain lots of sugar. For example, baked beans usually contain around 6% sugar and a can of coke contains 35 g of sugar (about 8 teaspoons worth). Sugar enters the bloodstream very <u>quickly</u>, making your blood sugar level <u>shoot up</u>. That's why it's better to eat <u>complex carbohydrates</u> (in brown bread, rice and cereals), which are broken down into sugar <u>gradually</u>.

2) Excess sugar in the body is converted into a <u>storage</u> carbohydrate called <u>glycogen</u> in the <u>liver</u>. If there's <u>too much</u> sugar for the liver to store it all as glycogen, it's converted into <u>fat</u> instead.

3) <u>Diabetes</u> is an illness that occurs when the body <u>can't</u> control its blood sugar levels properly. There are two types of diabetes, <u>type 1</u> and <u>type 2</u>.

4) <u>Poor diet</u> and <u>obesity</u> increase your risk of developing <u>type 2</u> (but <u>not</u> type 1) diabetes.

The Two Types of Diabetes Cause Problems in Different Ways

The two types of diabetes <u>develop</u> for different reasons and are <u>treated</u> in different ways.

TYPE 1

1) Type 1 diabetes usually develops in <u>young</u> people and happens when the <u>pancreas</u> stops producing <u>insulin</u>, for reasons that aren't fully understood yet.

2) Because the body can't produce insulin, it can't remove <u>sugar</u> from the blood and store it. Blood sugar levels can become so <u>high</u> that they damage the body, possibly even causing coma and death.

3) Type 1 diabetes is treated by <u>daily injections of insulin</u> and by controlling the <u>diet</u> to help control the blood sugar levels. It's important that diabetics don't miss meals, or the insulin they've injected could make their blood sugar levels drop too <u>low</u>, which can also be dangerous.

TYPE 2

1) Type 2 diabetes usually affects <u>older</u> people and symptoms develop gradually. They include weight loss, needing to wee often and tiredness. It can develop if the body stops making enough <u>insulin</u> because it can't respond properly to high blood sugar levels. Or the body might be producing enough insulin, but stops <u>responding</u> to it normally. Both these things are linked to a <u>poor diet</u> and <u>obesity</u>.

2) Type 2 diabetes is controlled by improving the <u>diet</u>, <u>losing weight</u> and <u>exercising regularly</u>. People with type 2 diabetes don't usually need a special diet, but it should be well-balanced and not too high in sugar to prevent sudden <u>surges</u> in blood sugar. Exercise also helps to keep the blood sugar level stable and helps prevent obesity. Sometimes insulin is also taken.

3) Type 2 diabetes is becoming more and more common in <u>young</u> people. This is because of increasing obesity due to poor diet and lack of exercise.

Just 8 spoonfuls of sugar leads to obesity and diabetes, lala...

One thing that they're keen on in science these days is <u>risk</u>, and this is just the kind of place they'd spring it on you. For example, what <u>risks</u> are associated with being <u>obese</u>? Why might people <u>accept</u> the risk involved in having a poor diet? (Think about stuff like <u>convenience</u>, <u>cost</u>, wide <u>availability</u> of processed foods.) You must be able to discuss <u>personal choices</u> in terms of <u>balancing</u> risk and benefit.

Harmful Chemicals in Food

You need to <u>eat</u> to live. But some foods can do you more <u>harm</u> than good...

Some Foods Are Dangerous Naturally...

Some plants contain <u>poisonous chemicals</u>, some are poisonous unless <u>cooked properly</u> and some cause <u>allergic reactions</u> in some people.

1) A lot of <u>mushrooms</u> are poisonous. Only a few are <u>deadly</u>, but many can cause <u>stomach upsets</u>.

2) <u>Cassava</u>, a plant found in South America, has a <u>floury root</u> that's widely eaten. In the root are compounds that produce lethal <u>cyanide</u> in the liver if eaten, but luckily it also contains a substance that <u>destroys</u> these compounds if it's <u>mixed</u> with them. This is normally done by either chopping up the roots and <u>boiling</u> them, or by <u>fermenting</u> them.

3) As many as one in 200 people are <u>allergic</u> to <u>proteins</u> found in <u>peanuts</u> and other nuts. In extreme cases this can be <u>fatal</u>, but more often the symptoms are a <u>rash</u> and <u>swelling</u> of the mouth and throat.

4) <u>Gluten</u>, a <u>protein</u> found in <u>wheat</u>, <u>rye</u> and <u>barley</u>, can cause <u>allergic reactions</u> in some people. Symptoms <u>vary</u> and may include rashes and swellings, stomach pain and vomiting, diarrhoea and bloating or even breathing problems. People with this allergy have to have a <u>gluten-free diet</u>.

...Others Contain Chemicals Left Over From Farming...

<u>Pesticides</u> and <u>herbicides</u> used in farming can be present in small amounts on <u>fruit</u> and <u>vegetables</u>.

1) These residues are usually in <u>very small amounts</u> and can be removed by careful <u>washing</u> and <u>peeling</u>.

2) The <u>long-term effect</u> on health of eating small amounts of these chemicals is not fully understood. The maximum recommended level for <u>baby foods</u> is particularly low and many people now feed their babies <u>organic</u> food. A recent study has linked residues with an increased risk of <u>Parkinson's disease</u> — a degenerative brain disease.

...Others Develop Dangerous Chemicals During Storage...

Some foods can contain harmful chemicals if they're not <u>stored</u> properly.

1) <u>Nuts</u>, <u>cereals</u> and <u>dried fruit</u> can become contaminated by a poisonous substance called <u>aflatoxin</u>.

2) Aflatoxin is produced by a <u>mould</u> that can grow on these foods if they're not stored correctly.

3) Aflatoxin can cause <u>liver cancer</u>.

4) <u>Bird seed</u> is a particular problem, as it doesn't have to meet the same <u>standards</u> as nuts for human consumption do. Birds and other animals can be <u>killed</u> if they eat contaminated seed.

...And Cooking Can Form Other Dangerous Chemicals

Chemicals that can be produced by burning foods include <u>polycyclic aromatic hydrocarbons (PAHs)</u>, and <u>heterocyclic amines (HAs)</u>.

1) Both PAHs and HAs can be formed when food is cooked at <u>high temperatures</u> (usually over 150 °C).

2) <u>HAs</u> are only formed in <u>meat</u> and <u>fish</u>, but PAHs may be formed in <u>other foods</u> too.

3) Both PAHs and HAs have been shown to cause <u>cancer</u> in animals by altering their <u>DNA</u>. <u>PAHs</u> are also known to cause cancer in <u>humans</u> — it's not known for sure whether HAs do, but it seems possible.

4) The amounts of PAHs and HAs produced can be <u>reduced</u> by choosing <u>lean</u> meat or fish, not letting <u>flames</u> touch the food and by cooking it at a <u>lower temperature</u> for longer.

Have you burnt the chicken again? — PAH! HA HA HA...

Here's that <u>risk and benefit</u> stuff again — scientists are <u>always</u> coming up with new ways that various foods are <u>bad</u> for us. But if you spend too much time analysing <u>all</u> those risks, you'd <u>never eat</u> at all.

Food Additives

You're not finished with food issues yet, I'm afraid. Here are all the chemicals that are put in on purpose.

Lots of Foods Contain Additives These Days

1) Food colours (should) make food look more appetising. They're often used in sweets and soft drinks. A place you might not expect to find food colouring is in mushy peas, which contain a green dye. Chocolate cake mixes often contain a brown food colouring (which you don't need in a proper home-made cake if you use enough cocoa powder).

2) Flavourings, fairly obviously, are added to foods to give them a new taste — e.g. adding an orange flavour to a soft drink. They could be extracted from a natural substance or made artificially. Flavour enhancers are a bit different — they bring out the taste and smell of food without adding a taste of their own (they're not flavourings as such). They're often added to ready meals.

3) Diet foods and drinks use artificial sweeteners like saccharin and aspartame instead of sugar. They taste sweeter than sugar so you don't have to use as much, making the products lower in calories.

4) When some foods react with oxygen, they go off. Oxygen can turn the fat in food into nasty-smelling and nasty-tasting substances — e.g. butter goes rancid when it's exposed to the air. Antioxidants are added to foods that contain fat or oil, e.g. sausages, to stop them reacting with oxygen.

5) Preservatives are added to many foods to prevent the growth of harmful microbes. The food can then be stored for longer before it goes off. A very common preservative is sodium benzoate, which is used in loads of foods including soft drinks and meat products.

Emulsifiers and Stabilisers Help Oils and Water Mix

1) You can mix an oil with water to make an emulsion. Emulsions are made up of lots of droplets of one liquid suspended in another liquid.

2) Oil and water naturally separate into two layers with the oil floating on top of the water — they don't "want" to mix. Emulsifiers help to stop the two liquids in an emulsion separating out.

3) Mayonnaise, low-fat spread and ice cream are foods which contain emulsifiers.

4) Stabilisers are added to foods to help emulsions stay mixed and to thicken them. They're added to lots of foods, e.g. ice cream, tomato sauce and many desserts.

The Use of Food Additives is Regulated

Food additives have to pass a safety test before they can be used.

1) In the EU (including the UK), all food additives have to pass a safety test and are then given an E number. Even oxygen has an E number, because it's used in gas-packed vegetables.

2) The standards set by the EU are different to those used in other countries. Some substances are allowed in the EU but not in other countries and vice-versa. For example, alkanet is a food colouring that isn't approved for use as a food additive in Europe (so it hasn't got an E number) but it is approved for use in Australia and New Zealand.

3) Despite these safety tests, some additives are still thought to cause health problems in some people. For example:

i) Some artificial food colourings have been linked with allergies and hyperactivity.

ii) Sulfur dioxide in dried fruit has been linked with asthma.

iii) Artificial sweeteners, e.g. aspartame, have been linked with hyperactivity and behavioural problems.

OK, enough — this is putting me off my chemical-filled lunch...

E numbers are something else that have had a very bad press lately. And fair enough, luminous coloured sweeties that have kids bouncing off the walls are probably a bit unnecessary. But some of the chemicals that are added are really useful, like preservatives that stop harmful microbes growing.

Keeping Food Safe

Reducing the risk of a hazard, e.g. a pesticide on food, costs money — it's expensive to remove the chemical, monitor the levels, etc. Governments have to balance the risks and costs to reach an acceptable level.

Foods Can Be Made Safer but Not Risk-free

Everything you do carries a certain amount of risk, even something as simple as eating a meal. New technology based on scientific advances introduces new risks, and these have to be limited.

1) For example, scientists genetically modify some crops to give them new characteristics, like better yields and resistance to diseases. However, some people are worried that this new technology might not be safe, and so any research into GM crops is strictly regulated. Any food that could contain GM plants must be clearly labelled so that consumers can avoid it if they'd prefer to.

2) Scientists are also responsible for many of the chemicals sprayed on or added to foods — e.g. herbicides and pesticides on crop plants, and flavourings and preservatives in processed foods. These have their advantages, but they also pose a risk (see p. 84). Governments and other organisations evaluate the risks on behalf of the rest of us, and impose laws and controls accordingly (see below).

3) No food can ever be guaranteed to be completely safe. There are too many stages in the food chain and too many different ways that a food could be contaminated. New allergies and food intolerances can develop at any point in a person's life. You simply have to accept a small amount of risk, and take what steps you can to make sure it's as low as possible.

4) For example, a lot can be done to reduce the potential risks of eating meat. The farmer should care for the animals properly. The animals should be slaughtered in a hygienic environment. The butcher must keep the meat in a clean and cold place, and members of the public should store and prepare the meat in the safest way. The government aims to ensure all this happens by licensing places like slaughterhouses, setting out guidelines, enforcing laws and educating the public.

> The 'precautionary principle' is an idea used by governments and individuals to help limit risks. For example, if you're not sure about some food, say unlabelled meat on a market stall in the sun, you shouldn't buy it unless you're prepared to accept the risk that it might be unsafe, however cheap it is. Basically, if you're not sure about something, and you know it could potentially cause serious harm, you'd best avoid it.

Scientists Decide Safe Levels of Chemicals in Food

Foods are regulated to make sure they don't pose a significant risk to health.

1) Chemicals get into food from a variety of sources and at every stage in the food supply chain — from pesticides in the fields, to processing, packaging and storage.

2) Scientific advisory committees, which aren't connected to the food industry, carry out risk assessments to help set safe limits for the levels of chemicals allowed in food.

3) The Food Standards Agency (FSA) is an independent food safety watchdog set up by an Act of Parliament to protect our health and consumer interests in relation to food.

4) The FSA offers advice to consumers and food producers on all aspects of food safety, labelling, diet, farming and hygiene. It also checks that legislation on these issues is being followed properly, for example by supporting food sampling programmes. These are carried out regularly by local authorities and involve testing various foods from different sources to make sure they're safe to eat.

©iStockphoto.com/Leah-Anne Thompson

I laugh in the face of danger — see, I haven't washed this pear...

I told you — these examiners love the whole idea of risk. In their spare time I expect they all go skydiving. This topic is an ideal way for them to introduce ideas about risk, but it's not the only place it could come up in an exam, so make sure you understand the general ideas behind these examples.

Eating Healthily

So the government and other organisations are keeping a beady eye on the companies and individuals producing our food, making sure they don't <u>poison</u> us. But lack of poison isn't the only component of a <u>healthy</u> diet.

Individual Choices Can Help Make Food Safer

Everyone should be aware of the <u>possible harmful effects</u> of <u>chemicals</u> in their food.
Individuals who want to <u>reduce</u> their exposure to potentially harmful chemicals can take several steps:

1) Choose food produced in a way that <u>minimises</u> the chemicals that are applied to it. This usually means eating <u>organic</u> food.
2) <u>Wash</u> the food carefully or <u>peel</u> it before eating it.
3) <u>Store</u> and <u>cook</u> the food in the way recommended on the packaging.

People can also use the <u>labels</u> on food to find out more about the consequences for their health.
Food labels now give <u>detailed information</u> such as the amounts of each <u>type of fat</u>, and sometimes whether this is high, medium or low compared with <u>other foods</u>.

The label should tell you <u>how</u> and <u>where</u> the food was produced, what it <u>contains</u> and whether it contains substances that people might be <u>allergic</u> to. Many also give you an idea of the <u>recommended daily amounts</u> of different substances you should be eating, and <u>how much</u> of that daily amount the product contains.

Choosing Food Isn't Just About What it Tastes Like

1) People <u>don't</u> all eat exactly the same diet. There's so much <u>choice</u> in countries like the UK now that one person's diet might be <u>completely different</u> to someone else's. One person might avoid fruit and vegetables altogether and live on junk food and processed ready meals, and another might be a vegan who eats a macrobiotic diet of organic foods.

2) More and more people <u>are</u> becoming concerned about the food that they eat, and many are turning to <u>organic</u> food. Organic food is often seen as <u>safer</u> because of the restrictions on the use of artificial chemicals. Some people also see it as more <u>natural</u> and <u>nutritious</u>. For these people, the potential <u>risks</u> posed by eating foods that have been grown on an intensive farm don't seem <u>worth</u> the benefits.

3) Don't forget, there <u>are</u> benefits to intensively grown foods. They're <u>cheaper</u>, and for people on lower incomes especially, this could be important. They often <u>look</u> more attractive, and because intensive farming methods are more widely used, there tends to be more <u>choice</u>.

4) There are also <u>advantages</u> to <u>processed ready meals</u> — for example, they're <u>quick</u> and <u>convenient</u>. For some people those benefits would outweigh the potential <u>risks</u> posed by the <u>additives</u> added to the food, the often high <u>sugar</u>, <u>fat</u> and <u>salt</u> contents, and so on.

5) All the food you can buy <u>has</u> been passed as <u>safe enough</u> to eat by the government, so unless you have an <u>allergy</u> to one of the ingredients, it's unlikely to <u>poison</u> you. This is enough for some people to dismiss all the risks of an unhealthy diet and eat just the things that they like.

6) Your diet is a personal choice, and each person <u>balances</u> the <u>risks</u> and <u>benefits</u> of eating different foods for themselves. Their <u>own opinions</u> and what they've learned from people around them and from the media will <u>influence</u> the balance they eventually decide on.

It's the Fast Food Giant versus Gillian McKeith...

I might write in and suggest they make a TV programme about that. Anyway, it's interesting that even though more and more people are eating <u>free range</u>, <u>organic</u>, <u>local</u>, <u>macrobiotic</u> and whatever, <u>obesity</u> is still one of the biggest killers in countries like the USA and UK. That's personal choice for you.

Revision Summary for Module C3

Okay, I'm sure you know what to do by now — and if by some chance you've forgotten, that great big list of questions should give you a clue. Go through and try them all, making a note of any you can't do. Then go back through the section and find the answers to the ones you were stuck on. And I warn you, if you don't try these questions, whenever you try to grow rhubarb it will not sprout, and whenever you make custard it will turn out lumpy.

1) How is dead animal and plant matter turned into compounds that plants can use?

2) Give three ways that nitrates are added to the soil in the nitrogen cycle.

3) Give two ways that nitrates are removed from the soil in the nitrogen cycle.

4) Explain why the nitrogen cycle does not happen in a field of crops.

5) Give three ways that organic farmers can replace the nutrients that are lost from their soil.

6) Give two advantages and two disadvantages of using artificial fertilisers on crops.

7) Give two ways that an organic farmer can limit the number of diseases affecting his or her crops.

8) Explain the advantages and disadvantages of using chemical pesticides to kill pests.

9) What must a farmer who grows crops and produces animals for meat do to be classed as organic?

10) Name two carbohydrate polymers. What is the name of the monomer that makes them up?

11) Which element is found in proteins but not in carbohydrates?

12) Name the monomer molecules that make up a protein polymer.

13) Why is starch in food broken down into glucose before being absorbed into the blood?

14) Give five ways that proteins are used in the body.

15) Where are excess amino acids broken down in the body? Where are they taken to be excreted?

16) What happens to excess sugar in the body?

17) How is type 1 diabetes usually treated?

18) Explain why type 2 diabetes is increasing in young people.

19) Explain why the South American plant, cassava, should not be eaten raw.

20) What is aflatoxin? What problem can it cause if eaten by humans?

21) What are PAHs and HAs? How can you limit your chance of eating them?

22) Why are the following added to food?   a) sodium benzoate   b) saccharin

23) Ice cream contains two different kinds of chemical to prevent it separating out — what are they?

24) Give two examples of problems caused by additives that have been passed as safe to use by the EU.

25)*Why can no food ever be guaranteed to be completely safe?

26) Explain what the 'precautionary principle' is.

27) Explain how scientific advisory committees and the **FSA** limit the risks posed by our food.

28) Suggest three ways that individuals can limit the risks posed by their food.

29) How can people make use of the labels on food to limit their risks?

30)*Outline some of the risks and benefits of eating intensively produced vegetables.

* Answers on page 104.

Radioactivity

Nuclear radiation — yet another type of radiation. But you do need to read these next few pages. Sorry.

Atoms Consist of a Nucleus Plus Orbiting Electrons

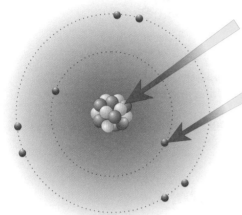

The nucleus contains protons and neutrons. It makes up most of the mass of the atom, but takes up virtually no space — it's tiny.

The electrons are really really small.
They whizz around the outside of the atom. Their paths take up a lot of space, giving the atom its overall size (though it's mostly empty space).

The Number of Neutrons in an Element isn't Fixed

1) Every atom of a particular element has the same number of protons in its nucleus, e.g. every carbon atom has 6 protons in its nucleus, every nitrogen atom has 7 protons in its nucleus, etc.

2) The number of neutrons isn't fixed, though. Many elements have a few different isotopes — atoms with the same number of protons but different numbers of neutrons.

3) E.g. there are two common isotopes of carbon — carbon-14 has two more neutrons than 'normal' carbon (carbon-12).

4) Usually each element only has one or two stable isotopes — like carbon-12.

5) The other isotopes tend to be radioactive — the nucleus is unstable, so it decays (breaks down) and emits radiation. Carbon-14 is an unstable isotope of carbon.

Carbon-12

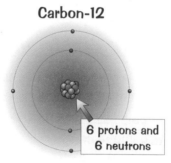

6 protons and 6 neutrons

Carbon-14

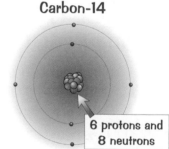

6 protons and 8 neutrons

Radioactive Elements Emit Nuclear Radiation

1) Radioactive atoms are unstable — they break up (decay) to make themselves more stable.

2) Unstable atoms decay at random. If you have 1000 unstable atoms, you can't say when any one of them is going to decay, and you can't do anything at all to make a decay happen.

3) Each atom just decays quite spontaneously in its own good time. It's completely unaffected by physical conditions like temperature or by any sort of chemical bonding etc.

4) When the atom does decay, it spits out one or more of the three types of radiation — alpha, beta and gamma (see p90).

5) In the process, the atom often changes into a new element.

Unstable isotopes — put them in a field...

So, it's the number of protons that decides what element something is (and so all its chemical properties). Then the number of neutrons decides what isotope of that element it is. Some isotopes of an element are stable, but others are unstable — it's the unstable ones that undergo radioactive decay.

The Three Kinds of Nuclear Radiation

There are three types of radiation — alpha (α), beta (β) and gamma (γ). You need to remember how well they penetrate materials and how a nucleus changes when they're emitted.

Alpha Radiation is Slow and Heavy

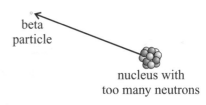

1) Alpha particles are relatively big and heavy and fairly slow-moving.
2) So they don't penetrate far into materials — they're stopped quickly.
3) Alpha particles are released by very heavy nuclei, e.g. uranium.
4) Alpha particles are made up of two protons and two neutrons. Alpha decay always changes the element of the atom doing the decaying, since the number of protons in its nucleus changes:

alpha particle

big unstable nucleus

E.g. uranium-238 is unstable. It decays by emitting an alpha particle to make itself more stable. This results in a new element — thorium-234 (which has two fewer protons than uranium).

Beta Radiation is Lighter and More Penetrating

1) Beta particles move quite fast and they are quite small.
2) They penetrate moderately into materials before they're stopped.
3) Beta particles are released by nuclei that have too many neutrons.
4) During beta decay, a neutron in the nucleus turns into a proton, so the element changes, and a beta particle is emitted.

beta particle

nucleus with too many neutrons

E.g. cobalt-60 decays by emitting a beta particle. This results in a new element — nickel-60 (which has one more proton in its nucleus than cobalt-60).

Gamma Radiation is an Electromagnetic Wave

1) After spitting out an alpha or beta particle, the nucleus might need to get rid of some extra energy. It does this by emitting a gamma ray.
2) Gamma rays are a type of EM radiation (see p.58) — they have no mass.
3) They can penetrate a long way into materials without being stopped.
4) Since a gamma ray is just energy, it doesn't change the element of the nucleus that emits it.

Remember What Blocks the Three Types of Radiation...

Alpha particles are blocked by paper.

Beta particles are blocked by thin aluminium.

Gamma rays are blocked by thick lead.

Of course anything equivalent will also block them, e.g. skin will stop alpha but not the others, a thin sheet of any metal will stop beta, and very thick concrete will stop gamma just like lead does.

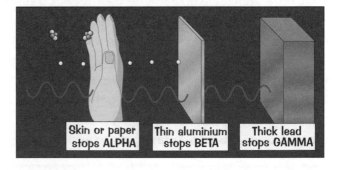

Skin or paper stops ALPHA

Thin aluminium stops BETA

Thick lead stops GAMMA

I once beta particle — it cried for ages...

So you can tell which kind of radiation you're dealing with by what blocks it. If it gets through paper, it could be either beta or gamma. If it gets through a sheet of aluminium, it must be gamma.

Half-Life

Radioactivity is measured in <u>becquerels</u> (<u>Bq</u>) or counts per minute (cpm). 1 Bq is one <u>decay per second</u>.

The Radioactivity of a Sample Always Decreases Over Time

1) Each time an unstable nucleus <u>decays</u> and emits radiation, that means one more <u>radioactive nucleus isn't there</u> to decay later.

2) As more <u>unstable nuclei</u> decay, the <u>radioactivity</u> of the source <u>as a whole decreases</u> — so the <u>older</u> a radioactive source is, the <u>less radiation</u> it emits.

3) <u>How quickly</u> the activity <u>decreases</u> varies a lot. For <u>some</u> isotopes it takes <u>just a few hours</u> before nearly all the unstable nuclei have <u>decayed</u>. For others it can take <u>millions of years</u>.

4) The problem with trying to <u>measure</u> this is that <u>the activity never reaches zero</u>, which is why we have to use the idea of <u>half-life</u> to measure <u>how quickly the activity decreases</u>.

5) Learn this <u>important definition</u> of <u>half-life</u>:

> **HALF-LIFE is the <u>TIME TAKEN</u> for <u>HALF</u> of the <u>radioactive atoms</u> now present to <u>DECAY</u>.**

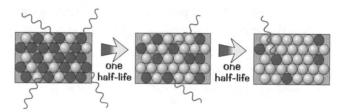

6) A <u>short half-life</u> means the <u>activity falls quickly</u>, because <u>lots</u> of the nuclei decay in a <u>short time</u>.

7) A <u>long half-life</u> means the activity <u>falls more slowly</u> because <u>most</u> of the nuclei don't decay <u>for a long time</u> — they just sit there, <u>basically unstable</u>, but kind of <u>biding their time</u>.

Do Half-Life Questions Step by Step

Half-life is maybe a little confusing, but exam calculations are <u>straightforward</u> so long as you do them slowly, <u>STEP BY STEP</u>. Like these two:

A VERY SIMPLE EXAMPLE:

The activity of a radioactive sample is 640 cpm.
Two hours later it has fallen to 40 cpm. Find the half-life of the sample.

<u>ANSWER</u>: Go through it in <u>short simple steps</u> like this:

INITIAL count:		after ONE half-life:		after TWO half-lives:		after THREE half-lives:		after FOUR half-lives:
640	(÷2) →	320	(÷2) →	160	(÷2) →	80	(÷2)→	40

This careful <u>step-by-step method</u> shows that it takes <u>four half-lives</u> for the activity to fall from 640 to 40. So <u>two hours</u> represents four half-lives — so the <u>half-life is 30 MINUTES</u>.

ANOTHER EXAMPLE:

Radium-226 has a half-life of 1620 years.
How long will it take for the count rate of a sample of radium-226 to drop from 10 Bq to 1.25 Bq?

<u>ANSWER</u>:

INITIAL count:		after ONE half-life:		after TWO half-lives:		after THREE half-lives:
10	(÷2) →	5	(÷2) →	2.5	(÷2) →	1.25

So, it takes <u>three half-lives</u> for the count rate to drop to 1.25 Bq.
Three half-lives is 3 × 1620 = <u>4860 YEARS</u>.

Half-life of a box of chocolates — about five minutes...

To measure half-life, you time how <u>long it takes</u> for the number of decays per second to halve — and this can vary from fractions of a second (you'd need to be mighty quick on the stopwatch) to thousands of millions of years (which is quite a while to wait with a Geiger counter and pencil).

Danger from Nuclear Radiation

Radioactive materials can be really useful, but they're also <u>dangerous</u> — they need <u>careful handling</u>.

Nuclear Radiation Causes Ionisation

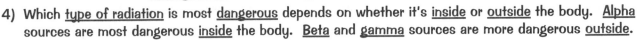

1) Alpha, beta and gamma radiation are all <u>ionising radiation</u> — they can <u>break up</u> molecules into smaller bits called <u>ions</u>. Ions can be <u>very chemically reactive</u>, so they go off and react with things and generally make <u>nuisances</u> of themselves.

2) In humans, ionisation can cause <u>serious damage</u> to the cells in the body.

3) A high dose of radiation tends to <u>kill cells</u> outright, causing <u>radiation sickness</u>. Lower doses tend to <u>damage cells</u> without killing them, which can cause <u>cancer</u>.

4) Which <u>type of radiation</u> is most <u>dangerous</u> depends on whether it's <u>inside</u> or <u>outside</u> the body. <u>Alpha</u> sources are most dangerous <u>inside</u> the body. <u>Beta</u> and <u>gamma</u> sources are more dangerous <u>outside</u>.

5) Radioactive materials put people at risk through either:

<u>IRRADIATION</u> — being exposed to radiation <u>without</u> coming into contact with the source. The damage to your body <u>stops</u> as soon as you leave the radioactive area.

<u>CONTAMINATION</u> — <u>picking up</u> some radioactive material, e.g. by <u>breathing it in</u>, <u>drinking</u> contaminated water or getting it on your skin. You'll <u>still</u> be exposed to the radiation once you've <u>left</u> the radioactive area.

Sieverts Show Possible Harm from Nuclear Radiation

1) How likely you are to <u>suffer damage</u> if you're exposed to nuclear radiation depends on the <u>radiation dose</u>. Radiation dose is measured in <u>sieverts</u> (<u>Sv</u>) or more usually <u>millisieverts</u> (<u>mSv</u>), and it takes into account the <u>type</u> and <u>amount of radiation</u> you've been exposed to, and the part of the body exposed.

2) The following data shows some <u>radiation doses</u> and their <u>effects</u> on the body:

2 mSv/year	Typical background radiation (see p.93) experienced by everyone.
9 mSv/year	Exposure by airline crew flying the New York to Tokyo polar route.
20 mSv/year	Current limit (averaged) for nuclear industry employees and uranium miners.
100 mSv/year	Lowest level at which an increase in cancer is clearly evident. Above this, the probability of cancer occurrence (rather than the severity) increases with dose.
1000 mSv/single dose	Causes (temporary) radiation sickness such as nausea and decreased white blood cell count, but not usually death. Above this, severity of illness increases with dose.
5000 mSv/single dose	Would kill about half of those receiving it within a month.
10 000 mSv/single dose	Fatal within a few weeks.

Researchers are still <u>arguing</u> about the effects of doses below 100 mSv/year, but most agree that a dose of 100 mSv per year for <u>10 years</u> <u>or more</u> will increase the risk of <u>cancer</u>.

Data from the World Nuclear Association

3) <u>Categories</u> of people who are at <u>higher risk</u> of radiation exposure include:

- <u>uranium</u> miners and processors
- workers in <u>nuclear power plants</u>
- <u>airline</u> staff (cosmic rays)
- <u>miners</u> (many rocks are naturally radioactive)
- some <u>medical</u> staff (e.g. radiographers)
- nuclear <u>researchers</u>

In Britain, people in high-risk industries have to <u>monitor</u> their radiation doses and have <u>regular check-ups</u>.

Revision sickness — never mind, only 7 pages to go...

Air hostesses — they should be wrapped head to toe in lead to keep the nasty radiation out, but because they wouldn't look as glam (and it'd cost the airlines too much money), they just get a silly hat.

Using Nuclear Radiation

We're constantly exposed to <u>very low levels</u> of radiation without us noticing — sneaky.

Background Radiation <u>is Everywhere</u> All the Time

There's low-level <u>background nuclear radiation</u> all around us all the time.

It comes from:

1) <u>NATURAL RADIOACTIVE SUBSTANCES</u> in the <u>air</u>, in <u>soil</u>, in <u>living things</u>, in the <u>rocks</u> under our feet...

2) <u>SPACE</u> (cosmic rays) — these come mostly from the <u>Sun</u>.

3) <u>HUMAN ACTIVITY</u> — e.g. from <u>nuclear explosions</u> or <u>waste from nuclear power plants</u>, although this is usually a <u>tiny</u> proportion (<1%) of the total background radiation.

<u>Radioactive sources</u> are considered to be "<u>safe</u>" when the radiation they are emitting is at about the <u>same level</u> as the <u>background radiation</u>. The <u>half-life</u> of the source gives an idea of how long it will take for this to happen. E.g. strontium-90 has a half-life of 29 years so a sample emitting 1000 cpm will take <u>four half-lives</u>, <u>116 years</u>, to reach roughly the background count of 60 cpm. (1000 cpm → 500 cpm → 250 cpm → 125 cpm → 62.5 cpm.)

Nuclear Radiation Can be <u>Very Useful</u> For...

...<u>Treating</u> Cancer

1) Since high doses of gamma rays will <u>kill all living cells</u>, they can be used to <u>treat cancers</u>.

2) The gamma rays have to be <u>directed carefully</u> and at just the right <u>dosage</u> so as to kill the <u>cancer cells</u> without damaging too many <u>normal cells</u>.

3) However, a <u>fair bit of damage</u> is <u>inevitably</u> done to <u>normal cells</u>, which makes the patient feel <u>very ill</u>. But if the cancer is <u>successfully killed off</u> in the end, then it's worth it.

...<u>Sterilising</u> Medical Equipment

1) Gamma rays are used to <u>sterilise</u> medical instruments by <u>killing</u> all the microbes.

2) This is better than trying to <u>boil</u> plastic instruments, which might be <u>damaged</u> by high temperatures. You need to use a <u>strongly</u> radioactive source that has a <u>long half-life</u>, so that it doesn't need replacing too often.

...<u>Sterilising</u> Food

1) <u>Food</u> can be sterilised in the same way as medical instruments — again <u>killing</u> all the <u>microbes</u>.

2) This keeps the food <u>fresh for longer</u>, without having to freeze it or cook it or preserve it some other way.

3) The food is <u>not</u> radioactive afterwards, so it's <u>perfectly safe</u> to eat.

Gamma radiation — just what the doctor ordered...

Like many scientific discoveries, background radiation was discovered <u>accidentally</u>. Scientists were trying to work out which materials were radioactive, and couldn't understand why their detector showed radioactivity when there was <u>no material</u> being tested. They were picking up background radiation.

Radiation and Risk

Nothing in life is completely safe. Scientific developments always bring new risks, e.g. new medicines can have nasty side effects, nuclear power stations might leak radioactive material.

We're More Willing to Take Some Risks Than Others

There are two separate parts to riskiness — the chances of something happening and how serious the consequences would be if it did.

The chances of a modern nuclear power station exploding are very low, but the consequences would be very serious if it did — many people would die and vast areas of land would be contaminated with radioactive material for years.	The chances of a small amount of radioactive material leaking from a nuclear power station are much higher. But, the consequences aren't so bad — often the contamination can be cleaned up (on land) or it gets diluted (in the sea or air) and so doesn't cause much harm.

1) Most of us are happy to take a risk if we know we're getting a substantial benefit.
   E.g. to help diagnose a medical condition, a patient might have radioactive material injected into their body as a tracer. This increases the patient's chances of developing cancer (very slightly) — but getting an accurate diagnosis (and then treatment) is a big benefit.

2) Our perception of risk (how risky we think things are) is often not very accurate.

Many people wouldn't want to live near a nuclear power plant because they think the background radiation level will be higher because of leaks.	The same people might be quite happy to live in Cornwall, even though background radiation is higher there (because of high levels of natural radon gas) than around most nuclear plants.

3) Many factors affect how we perceive risk, e.g. more 'dramatic' events make news — leaks from nuclear plants are usually reported by the media, but radon gas seeping into people's homes is not.

Nuclear Industries Use the ALARA and Precautionary Principles

1) Working with radiation always has some risks attached to it — but the aim should be to keep the risks As Low As Reasonably Achievable — using the ALARA principle (see p.4).
   - E.g. when radioactive materials are used as medical tracers, just enough radioactive material is used to give a reliable trace, so as to keep the patient's radiation dose as low as possible.

2) The precautionary principle means assuming the worst and taking appropriate action.
   - E.g. in nuclear power plants, even in parts of the building where there's no radioactive material, you have to wear protective clothing and get scanned by a radiation detector when you leave. There's almost certainly no contamination — but you assume there is and take precautions anyway.

There are laws that set down minimum safety precautions that have to be taken with radioactive materials.

Using Radioactive Materials Brings Both Risks and Benefits

Risky activities have benefits (and risks) for different groups of people.
For example, in building and running a new nuclear power station:

1) Construction companies benefit from years of work in building the power station.

2) Local people benefit from new jobs — but might suffer from higher radiation exposure.

3) The national population benefits from a reliable source of electricity — but is at some risk.

4) There's a global benefit because nuclear power contributes a lot less to climate change than burning fossil fuels — but there's a global risk too, from a major accident like the Chernobyl disaster.

Revise well — reduce the risk of exam failure...

Most of us prefer to risk more likely hazards with less serious consequences. E.g. we're quite happy to use sharp knifes and risk cutting our finger, but won't do a parachute jump and risk a broken neck.

Module P3 — Radioactive Materials

Electricity

A slight diversion for a few pages, but you'll be reading about nuclear radiation again soon enough.

Electricity is a Convenient Way to Supply Energy

1) Electricity is a secondary energy source because it is produced using other energy resources e.g. by burning coal, nuclear reactions.

2) Electricity is convenient because it can be easily transmitted over long distances via the National Grid, and can be used in many different ways.

3) Power stations are used to generate electricity in three stages:

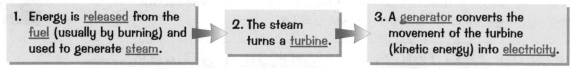

1. Energy is released from the fuel (usually by burning) and used to generate steam.

2. The steam turns a turbine.

3. A generator converts the movement of the turbine (kinetic energy) into electricity.

Supplying Electricity isn't Close to 100% Efficient

1) Unfortunately, most power stations aren't very efficient. They produce lots of waste energy (heat and noise) as well as useful electricity. Some energy is also lost as heat in the transmission wires as the electricity is distributed from the power station to people's homes.

2) Sankey diagrams let you see at a glance how much of the input energy is being usefully employed, and how much wasted.

3) The thicker the arrow, the more energy it represents — so you see a big thick arrow going in, then several smaller arrows going off it to show the different energy transformations.

4) The width of each arrow is proportional to the amount of energy it represents (measured in joules in this case).

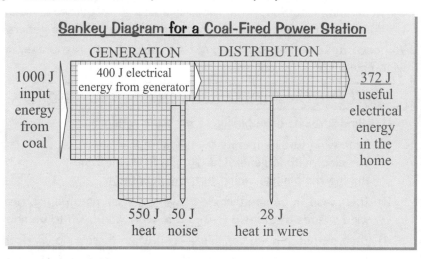

Sankey Diagram for a Coal-Fired Power Station

GENERATION   DISTRIBUTION

1000 J input energy from coal

400 J electrical energy from generator

372 J useful electrical energy in the home

550 J heat   50 J noise   28 J heat in wires

5) You can calculate the efficiency of the energy transfers shown in the diagram using this equation:

$$\text{Efficiency} = \frac{\text{USEFUL Energy OUTPUT}}{\text{Energy INPUT}}$$

Efficiency of GENERATION: $\text{Efficiency} = \dfrac{\text{electricity energy from generator}}{\text{energy input from coal}} = \dfrac{400}{1000} = \underline{0.4}$

Efficiency of DISTRIBUTION: $\text{Efficiency} = \dfrac{\text{useful electrical energy output}}{\text{electricity energy from generator}} = \dfrac{372}{400} = \underline{0.93}$

OVERALL efficiency: $\text{Efficiency} = \dfrac{\text{useful electrical energy output}}{\text{energy input from coal}} = \dfrac{372}{1000} = \underline{0.372}$

Skankey diagrams — to represent the smelliness of your socks...

The thing about loss of energy is it's always the same — whatever the process, some energy always disappears as heat and sound, and even the sound ends up as heat pretty quickly.

Generating Electricity

Most UK electricity comes from fossil-fuel power stations that burn either coal, oil or natural gas.
The Government target is to have <u>10%</u> of our electricity generated from <u>renewable resources</u> by 2010.

Fossil Fuel _Power Stations Release_ Carbon Dioxide — _Not Ideal_

1) At the moment, nearly three quarters of all the electricity generated in the UK comes from <u>fossil fuels</u> (<u>oil</u>, <u>gas</u> and <u>coal</u>) — which all contain <u>carbon</u>.

2) When fossil fuels are burned in power stations, the carbon is converted into <u>carbon dioxide</u>.

3) This carbon dioxide is released into the atmosphere and contributes to the <u>greenhouse effect</u> and climate change (see p.63-65).

Renewable _Energy Resources are an Alternative_

1) Renewable resources include <u>wind</u>, <u>solar</u>, <u>biomass</u>, <u>wave</u>, <u>tidal</u>, <u>hydroelectric</u> and <u>geothermal</u> energy.

2) These will <u>never run out</u>.

3) If they damage the environment, they tend to do it in <u>less nasty ways</u> than fossil fuels.

4) The trouble is they <u>don't yet provide much energy</u> and some of them are <u>unreliable</u> because they depend on the weather.

5) Generating electricity from renewable energy resources is an example of <u>sustainable development</u> — it doesn't cause damage which harms the ability of future generations to meet their needs.

You need to know <u>two examples</u> of renewable energy resources, so here are a few more details about wind power and solar power:

Wind Power — _Lots of Little_ Wind Turbines

1) Wind turbines have <u>blades</u>, a bit like a <u>windmill</u>.

2) Each wind turbine has its own <u>generator</u> inside it. The electricity is generated <u>directly</u> from the wind turning the <u>blades</u>, which <u>turn the generator</u>.

3) They need to be sited where it's <u>windy</u>, such as on a <u>hill</u>, near the <u>coast</u> or <u>off-shore</u>. They need wind speeds of at least 3-4 m/s to work and have to be shut down if conditions get too stormy.

4) Their output is quite <u>variable</u> — and when there's <u>no wind</u>, there's <u>no power</u> at all.

5) But there are <u>no carbon dioxide</u> emissions, and <u>no fuel costs</u> (wind is free).

6) At the moment wind energy contributes about <u>1%</u> to the UK's overall electricity generation. This is likely to increase over the next 10 years to help meet targets on reducing carbon dioxide emissions.

Solar Power — _Electricity from the Sun_

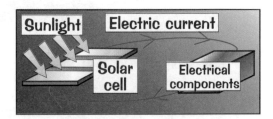

1) Solar cells use special materials like <u>silicon</u> which can convert light energy into electricity <u>directly</u>.

2) They're often the best source of energy for appliances which don't use much energy (e.g. calculators), and in <u>remote areas</u> where there aren't many other options.

3) Solar energy can only be generated <u>during the day</u>, and ideally you need <u>plenty of sunshine</u>. Some of the electricity can be used to <u>charge a battery</u> for use during the night.

4) As with wind power, there are <u>no carbon dioxide</u> emissions, and <u>no fuel costs</u>.

Solar cells are like fried eggs — best sunny side up...

If you have your own solar panel or wind turbine, you can <u>sell back</u> any surplus electricity to the National Grid. So if you don't use much electricity but you <u>generate</u> a lot of it, you can actually make money instead of spending it. Nice trick if you can do it. Shame solar panels cost an arm and a leg...

Electricity from Nuclear Fuels

Nuclear power stations can make <u>lots of energy</u> <u>without</u> releasing lots of CO_2 into the atmosphere. Some people think nuclear power is the <u>best</u> way to reduce CO_2 emissions, but others think it's just <u>too dangerous</u>.

Nuclear **Power Stations Release Energy by** *Splitting Atoms*

1) A <u>nuclear fuel</u>, e.g. <u>uranium</u>, releases large amounts of energy when its nuclei <u>undergo changes</u>.

2) In <u>nuclear fission</u>, neutrons are fired at the uranium, causing some of its nuclei to split into two smaller nuclei of roughly equal size. Each split nucleus also releases 2 or 3 more neutrons and <u>lots of energy</u>.

3) The uranium is contained in cylindrical metal tubes called <u>fuel rods</u>.

Nuclear Fission **Releases a** <u>Lot</u> **of Energy...**

Nuclear reactions release <u>a lot more energy</u> than chemical reactions (like burning, say). For every <u>gram</u> of <u>uranium</u> split, over <u>10 000 times</u> more energy is released than from a <u>gram</u> of <u>oil</u> being burnt.

...So It Needs to be *Carefully Controlled*

1) In nuclear reactors, a <u>chain reaction</u> is set up. A neutron splits a uranium atom, releasing more neutrons. These can then go on to split more uranium atoms and release more neutrons...

2) This chain reaction has to be <u>controlled</u>, or the reactor would overheat.

3) <u>Control rods</u> <u>absorb</u> some of the <u>neutrons</u> and slow down the reaction. They can be moved further into and out of the reactor to absorb more or less neutrons.

4) <u>Water</u> or <u>carbon dioxide</u> is used as a <u>coolant</u> to take away the heat produced by the fission process. This heat is used to produce <u>steam</u> to drive a <u>turbine</u> and <u>generator</u>.

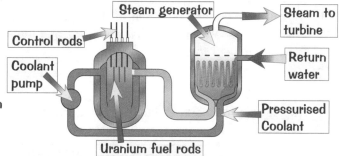

The <u>Waste</u> **from Nuclear Power Stations is** <u>Hard to Deal With</u>

Some people argue that nuclear power is <u>not a sustainable</u> technology — because it produces dangerous <u>radioactive waste</u> which will be a problem for future generations.

1) Most waste from nuclear power stations is '<u>low level</u>' (slightly radioactive) — e.g. things like paper, clothing, gloves, etc. This kind of waste can be disposed of by <u>burying</u> it in secure landfill sites.

2) <u>Intermediate level</u> waste includes things like the metal cases of used fuel rods. It's usually quite radioactive — and some of it will stay that way for <u>tens of thousands</u> of years. It's often sealed into <u>concrete blocks</u> then put in <u>steel canisters</u> for storage.

3) <u>High level</u> waste is <u>so radioactive</u> that it generates a lot of <u>heat</u>. This waste is sealed up in <u>glass</u> and steel, then <u>cooled</u> for about 50 years before it can be moved to more permanent storage.

4) The canisters of intermediate and high level wastes <u>could</u> then be buried <u>deep</u> underground. However, it's difficult to find <u>suitable places</u>. The site has to be <u>geologically stable</u> (e.g. not suffer earthquakes), since big movements in the rock could <u>break</u> the canisters and radioactive material could <u>leak out</u>.

5) Even when geologists <u>do</u> find suitable sites, people who live nearby often object. So, at the moment, most intermediate and high level waste is kept 'on-site' at nuclear power stations.

6) There are very strict regulations about how radioactive waste is disposed of. But the rules could <u>change</u> as we find out more about the dangers of radiation, and the pros and cons of storing waste in different ways. What's allowed now might be considered <u>too risky</u> in the future.

Nuclear power — people tend to get steamed up about it...

Building lots of nuclear power stations would mean we wouldn't have to rely on fossil fuels — and we wouldn't have to buy so much fuel from other countries. But do the <u>risks</u> outweigh the <u>benefits</u>...

Electricity in the Future

No Energy Source is Perfect

The table below shows comparison data for some large, modern power stations in the UK:

	Coal	Natural gas	Nuclear	Wind
Efficiency	36%	60%	38%	60%
Energy output per year (millions of units)	8000	5000	7000	150
CO_2 emissions per unit of electricity (g)	920	440	110	none
Lifetime of the site (years)	50	30	25	25
Cost of energy per unit	2.5-4.5p	2-3p	4-7p	3-4p

Talking about the efficiency of a wind farm doesn't mean all that much, though, since the 'fuel' is free and renewable.

The CO_2 emissions figures include the CO_2 released by mining and transporting the fuel, as well as burning it.

We Have to Look for the Best Compromise

We Need a Steady, Reliable Fuel Supply

1) All our uranium and over half of the coal we burn is currently imported from other countries. This makes us dependent on other countries and means transport costs and transport-related CO_2 emissions need to be considered.

2) Our supply of coal, oil and gas will probably run out within 50 years or so, and uranium will run out eventually.

3) Renewable fuel sources such as wind, tides, solar and water are free and won't run out. But some of them are quite variable — it's not always sunny and the wind doesn't blow all the time.

We Need Enough Electricity... Obviously

The UK uses a lot of electricity. Renewable resources struggle to produce the same sort of energy output as conventional power stations. E.g. it would take 800 of the biggest, top-of-the-range wind turbines to provide the same amount of energy as Drax (the UK's biggest coal-fired power station).

We Need to Keep the Environmental Impact Down

1) Reducing carbon dioxide emissions (and other pollutants from fossil fuels) is a high priority.

2) Some energy resources directly affect wildlife habitats more than others. E.g. tidal barrages and most hydroelectric power (HEP) schemes work by damming water — this floods the land, destroying habitats. Wind farms take up a lot more room than other types of power station, but the land in between the turbines can be used.

3) Nuclear energy has different environmental impacts from other fuels. The mining of uranium leaves a lot of waste material, including radioactive rock and toxic metals. The decommissioning of a nuclear power station takes about 25 years, and how to get rid of nuclear waste hasn't been resolved yet.

4) Noise pollution is another consideration. Wind farms can be quite noisy close up, so some people don't want them near their homes. Coal-fired plants need to be supplied with coal, which can mean heavy traffic and the noise that goes with it.

5) And visual pollution. Conventional power stations are generally considered unattractive. Some people also find wind turbines ugly, and the best sites for HEP are often in areas of natural beauty.

Of course the biggest problem is that we use too much electricity...

It would be lovely if we could get rid of all the nasty polluting power stations and replace them with clean, green fuel... but it's not quite that simple. Renewable energy has its own problems too, and probably couldn't power the whole country without having a wind farm in everyone's backyard.

Revision Summary for Module P3

Phew... what a relief — you made it to the end of yet another section. But don't run off to put the kettle on just yet — make sure that you really know your stuff with these revision questions.

1) What are the three particles found in an atom? Which two are found in the nucleus?
2) What do we mean by an 'unstable' atom?
3) Oxygen contains 8 protons. What is the difference between oxygen-16 and oxygen-18?
4) Radioactive decay is spontaneous. Explain what this means.
5) Describe the nature and properties of the three types of radiation: α, β and γ.
6) What substances could be used to block: a) α-radiation, b) β-radiation, c) γ-radiation?
7) Define half-life.
8)* The activity of a radioactive sample is 840 cpm. Four hours later it has fallen to 105 cpm. Find the half-life of the sample.
9) Describe what kind of damage radiation causes to body cells. What are the effects of high doses? What are the effects of lower doses?
10) What units are doses of radiation measured in? What three things does 'dose' take into account?
11) Give four categories of people who are at a higher than normal risk of exposure to radiation.
12) Give three sources of background nuclear radiation.
13) Describe in detail how radioactive sources are used in each of the following:

    a) treating cancer, b) sterilising medical equipment, c) sterilising food.

14) Suggest a reason why someone might be willing to expose themselves to nuclear radiation, despite the known risks associated with it.
15) In the context of radioactive materials, explain:

    a) the ALARA principle, b) the precautionary principle.

16) Outline arguments for and against the building of a nuclear power plant.
17) What is a secondary energy source? Give an example.
18) Describe the three stages by which power stations generate electricity.
19)* The following Sankey diagram shows how energy is converted in a coal-fired power station.

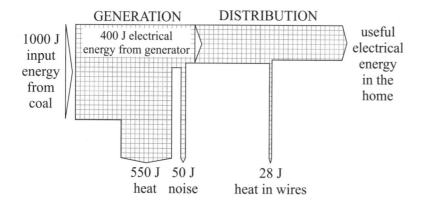

a) How much energy is converted into useful electrical energy in the home?

b) How much energy is wasted?

c) What is the overall efficiency?

20) Name three types of renewable energy resource.
21) Give one advantage and one disadvantage of using: a) wind power, b) solar power.
22) Describe how nuclear power stations generate electricity using uranium fuel.
23) What are the main environmental problems associated with nuclear power?

* Answers on page 104.

Dealing With Tricky Questions

So, you've made it to the end of the book — well done. I'm afraid that's not quite it though... you've still got the small matter of your exams to sort out.

The Exams for Units 1, 2 and 3 are Fairly Straightforward

Most of the questions you'll get in the exam will be pretty straightforward, as long as you've learnt your stuff. But there are a few things you need to be aware of that could catch you out...

A Lot of Questions will be Based on Real-Life Situations...

...so learn to live with it.

All they do is ask you how the science you've learned fits into the real world — that's all.

That equation you learned still works... and that graph is still the same shape.

Don't worry that the theory you've learned might not apply in different situations. IT WILL. For example...

> 4. European adders are found in a range of different colours from light brown to black.
>
> What are the possible causes of this variation?

It doesn't matter if you don't know anything about adders (who does?). You just need to apply the stuff you've learned about the genetic and environmental causes of variation.

There are Loads of Tick the Box Questions

The examiners seem fairly keen on questions where you have to choose from options by ticking boxes.

First things first — is it 'TICK' or 'TICKS'?
Check whether you can tick more than one box...

Then look through your options and use what you know to rule out the wrong 'uns.

You're only looking for one right answer.

One of the big things about chemical reactions is that none of the atoms just disappear so this sounds unlikely.

Hmm, this doesn't sound right when you think about it. Sometimes the products of a reaction are in a different state from the reactants so they're unlikely to have the same properties.

This one's pretty much the opposite of the first and fourth ones — and since we've decided they're wrong this one seems like a pretty good bet.

This one is saying something similar to the first one — that the total number of atoms changes during the reaction. We've already ruled that out.

> 5. The equation shows the reaction between sodium and chlorine
>
> $$2Na + Cl_2 \rightarrow 2NaCl$$
>
> Which of the following statements applies to the equation?
> Put a tick in the correct box.
>
> The product contains 50% less chlorine than the reactants. ☐
>
> The product is likely to have the same properties as the reactants. ☐
>
> The amount of sodium in the reactants and the product is equal. ☑
>
> Most of the atoms in the product were not originally in the reactants. ☐

If at first you don't succeed — come back to it later...

It's true — you might get a stinker in the exam. So, do the straightforward ones first and then come back to the tricky ones when you've done your best with the rest of the paper.*

Extract Questions

There might be a question on the exam where you have to answer questions about a <u>chunk of text</u>. If there is, here's what to do....

Questions with Extracts can be Tricky

1) Nowadays, the examiners want you to be able to <u>apply</u> your scientific knowledge to situations you've <u>never seen</u> before. Eeek.

2) The trick is <u>not</u> to <u>panic</u>. They're <u>not</u> expecting you to show Einstein-like levels of scientific insight (not usually, anyway).

3) They're just expecting you to use the science you <u>know</u> in an <u>unfamiliar setting</u> — and usually they'll give you some <u>extra info</u> too that you should use in your answer.

So to give you an idea of what to expect come exam time, use the new <u>CGP Exam Simulator</u> (below). Read the article and have a go at the questions. It's <u>guaranteed</u> to be just as much fun as the real thing.

Underlining or making notes of the main bits as you read is a good idea.

1. Blood glucose levels controlled by insulin.

2. Insulin added → liver removes glucose.

3. Not enough insulin → high blood glucose → death?

4. Two key methods involved in managing the problem

5. New areas of research - hopes for new treatments

This question is similar to the one on the opposite page — the best approach is to eliminate the definite 'nos' and then see what you have left. The article should give you some clues.

For this one you need to apply the arguments for and against embryonic research to the situation in the article.

All cells need energy to function, and this energy is supplied by glucose carried in the blood. The level of glucose in the blood is controlled by the hormone <u>insulin</u> — if the <u>blood glucose level gets too high, insulin is</u> introduced into the bloodstream by the pancreas, which in turn makes the <u>liver</u> remove glucose from the blood.

Diabetes (type I) is where <u>not enough insulin is produced</u>, meaning that a person's blood <u>glucose level can rise to a level that can kill them</u>. The problem can be controlled using a combination of these methods:

a) Avoiding foods rich <u>in carbohydrates</u>. It can also be helpful to take <u>exercise</u> after eating carbohydrates.

b) <u>Injecting</u> insulin before meals.

At a recent press conference, Dave Edwards from InsulinProducts plc said, "We have invested heavily in <u>embryonic stem cell</u> research and expect to be launching the final phase of our <u>testing into replacing</u> pancreas cells over the next year. We're <u>confident</u> that treatments for <u>diabetes</u> will change dramatically within the next decade. We believe that our research will improve the lives of the many diabetics who suffer daily and further our scientific understanding".

(a) People with diabetes should eat sensibly after injecting insulin. Put a tick in a box to show the **best** explanation of this.*

The insulin will cause their glucose levels to increase too rapidly. ☐

The insulin will remove glucose from their blood — if no food is eaten the blood sugar level may drop too low. ☐

The insulin could damage their liver. ☐

The insulin will remove salt from their blood — if no food is eaten the salt levels could fall too much. ☐

(b) Put a ring around the sentence that provides a justification for research using embryos.*

Thinking in an exam — it's not like the old days...

*Answers on page 104

It's scary when they expect you to <u>think</u> in the exam. But questions like this often have some of the answers <u>hidden</u> in the text, which is always a bonus. Just make sure you read <u>carefully</u> and take your <u>time</u>.

Interpreting Data

Chances are there'll be a few <u>data-related</u> questions of some kind in your exam — graphs, tables, that kind of thing. Here's an example to show you what you need to be able to do.

Get as Much Practice as You Can at Reading Graphs

The idea of graphs is to make <u>data</u> easier to <u>interpret</u>. And that's <u>generally true</u> — but they can be tricky.

So try to get <u>lots of practice</u> at reading graphs before the exam. And as I've said before, if you get one in the exam, <u>don't panic</u>.

Libby finds this graph in a newspaper article on modern life and climate change.

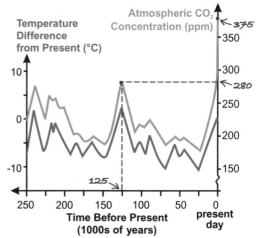

Tick the correct box for each of these questions.

Finding a Value — Make Sure You're Reading the Right Scale

Start by finding the CO_2 <u>line</u> — the <u>green</u> one — then find its <u>highest point</u> before the present day. <u>Draw a line</u> down to the "<u>Time Before Present</u>" scale and read off the number: <u>125</u>.

But <u>BEWARE</u> — the scale is in <u>thousands of years</u>, so it's <u>125 000 years ago</u>, not 125.

(a) When was the atmospheric CO_2 concentration at its highest before the recent increase?

AD 125 ☐

240 000 years ago ☐

125 years ago ☐

125 000 years ago ☑

Interpreting Data — Be Careful What You Assume

Be careful that your conclusions <u>match</u> the data you've got, and <u>don't</u> go any further. You can see that this graph shows a pretty close <u>correlation</u> between <u>temperature</u> and <u>carbon dioxide</u> level. <u>But that's all</u>.

The graph <u>can't</u> tell you what's <u>causing</u> the correlation. This is <u>not</u> a <u>controlled</u> experiment in a lab — so there are probably <u>other factors</u> at work. It could be that temperature controls the CO_2 level, or maybe it's the other way round. Or maybe <u>another factor</u> that's not shown on the graph is affecting both.

So you have to rule out the second and last ones, whether you think they're true or not.

The <u>best conclusion</u> you can draw is that <u>as one changes, the other changes</u> as well — that's true whatever the cause. So the third one is the best answer.

(b) What conclusion can you draw from this graph?

There is no relationship between the carbon dioxide level and temperature. ☐

A rise in temperature causes a rise in the carbon dioxide level. ☐

The temperature rises and falls as the carbon dioxide level rises and falls. ☑

Humans are causing the temperature to rise by emitting too much carbon dioxide. ☐

Graphs are like MPs — they don't give you the whole picture...

There's not too much argument about the 'more CO_2 is making us warmer' theory now (although there <u>was</u> plenty of doubt previously, when the data was dodgy). But some people do still question whether the warming is <u>our fault</u> or just down to <u>natural variability</u> in the climate. Nothing's ever simple. Sigh.

Exam Skills — Paper Four

You've got to do an exam that's a bit out of the ordinary — Paper Four, Ideas In Context. As I've said a few times over the last few pages DON'T WORRY about it, just calmly read through this page and then DO EXACTLY WHAT I SAY.

You'll be Given Some Material in Advance

Before the exam you'll be given a booklet containing some articles that you'll be examined on. Don't just stuff it in the bottom of your bag with your PE kit — start working on it straight away.

The articles could be on any science topic that's related to the material on the specification. They could well be about something that's been in the news recently, or you could get an article about how scientific understanding has developed over time.

So, don't be surprised if some of them seem a bit wacky — they will be related to the stuff you've learned — it might just take you a while to figure out how...

Start work as soon as you get the booklet

1) Read all the articles carefully and slowly — take your time and make sure you understand everything.

2) Look up any words that you don't know.

3) If there are any graphs, tables or figures in the articles then study them carefully. Identify any trends and make sure you know what they show (see opposite for more on this).

4) You don't need to do any extra research on the topics but if you're struggling with the material then a bit of extra reading might help you to understand it — try textbooks and internet searches. Don't get too carried away though — you shouldn't need any extra knowledge to answer the questions.

5) Although you don't need to do research you do need to make sure you've revised the topics that the articles are about. So if there's one about cystic fibrosis make sure you've revised genes, genetic inheritance and all the stuff about stem cells and gene therapy.

6) Remember to do all of the above for all of the articles — you'll have to answer questions on all of them in the exam.

7) It's a good idea to highlight important things in the booklet and make some notes as you go along, but remember that you can't take the booklet into the exam.

There'll be a mixture of questions in the exam

When you get to the exam you'll be given another copy of the articles, and some questions to go with them.

1) For some of the questions you'll need to extract information from the articles (see page 101).

2) Other questions will be about analysing data or information in the articles (see page 102).

3) Other questions will ask you about related topics from the specification — but you won't be expected to know anything that isn't on the specification or in the article.

I'd prefer an exam where you get the questions in advance...

The trick with this paper is to use the time before the exam to make sure you're really comfortable with the topics that are covered in the articles. If you're the type who watches the news and stuff then chances are you'll be familiar with some of the issues before you even get the booklet.

Answers

Revision Summary for Module B1 (page 17)

8) A person's sex cells are not all identical — each contains a random allocation of alleles. Each child inherits genetic material that's different from that of its siblings (and other children) as they're created from different sex cells. Only identical twins are formed from the same sperm and egg, so only they inherit exactly the same DNA.

11)
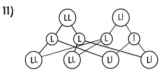

Revision Summary for Module C1 (page 27)

19) Results may be inaccurate, perhaps because of experimental error, inaccurate instruments, or values changing.

20) E.g. an increase in air pollution, higher pollen levels, an increase in infections like colds or flu, higher emotional stress levels, an inhaler shortage.

Revision Summary for Module P1 (page 38)

10) Currently, we don't understand well enough what 'warning signs' to look for to be able to say, reliably, when and where a jolt will happen. Strains in rocks only suggest an earthquake is more likely, not that it is certain.

23) The 'scientific community' (all the scientists working in the same field) judges whether a theory should be accepted or rejected by pointing out flaws, repeating the experiments, etc. If the theory stands up to this scrutiny, it's accepted.

'Peer review' means that when a scientist has done some research and written a report about it, another scientist working in the same field reads the report before it's published. This 'reviewer' checks that the experiments have been conducted properly and written up in a detailed and unbiased way, and looks for any obvious flaws.

Revision Summary for Module B2 (page 48)

8) The inactive microbes still carry antigens which your immune system recognises — so your white blood cells produce antibodies to attack them. If you're infected with the same disease, these white blood cells can reproduce rapidly and release lots of antibodies to kill off the micoorganisms before you become ill.

14) If almost everybody is vaccinated against a disease, even those who aren't vaccinated won't get the disease (there are probably no infected people around them to pass the microorganisms on). However, fears about side effects could lead people to stay unvaccinated. Then if just one or two people caught the disease, there would be other non-vaccinated people to catch it, then pass it on to others, etc.

Revision Summary for Module C2 (page 57)

10a) 3.4 and 14.2 (the anomalous results)

b) 8.1 + 8.3 + 8.1 + 8.0 + 8.3 + 8.4 + 8.0 + 8.2 = 65.4

65.4 ÷ 8 = 8.175 = 8.2 g/cm³ (to 1 d.p.)

13) Any three from: non-toxic, stiff, non-brittle, hard, fairly high melting point.

Revision Summary for Module P2 (page 67)

22) There could be health risks from heating tissues, e.g. in the brain. The amount of heating depends on the intensity of the radiation and the exposure time. Mobile phones emit fairly low intensity radiation, but are held close to the head — the intensity doesn't decrease much over this short distance. If you use a phone for a long time, you're exposed to more radiation, increasing the heating effect.

38) Any sensible explanation of how a factor causes an outcome.

Revision Summary for Module B3 (page 77)

6) No. Only features which help organisms to survive and pass on their genes (to a greater extent than individuals without the feature) are 'naturally selected'.

11) A geographical barrier would keep two groups of the same species isolated. An individual with a beneficial mutation would have offspring which lived in just one group. The same mutation would be unlikely to occur in an individual in the other group, so the change would be passed on in one group only. Over time, both groups might change in so many different ways that they'd be classed as different species altogether.

29) There'd be nothing to eat. Also, ecosystems would become unstable and less able to resist, and recover from, damage. Biodiversity is also important in the search for new medicines.

Revision Summary for Module C3 (page 88)

25) There are many ways that the food could have become accidentally contaminated (e.g. with pesticides and herbicides). You can't predict with absolute certainty your body's reaction to it. High temperature cooking can produce PAHs and HAs.

30) The risks mainly concern the chemicals used in the production of these foods. By law, residues of pesticides, etc. should only exist in small amounts, but nobody is certain of the long-term effect of eating small amounts repeatedly. Some residues have been linked with diseases e.g. Parkinson's. Fertiliser washing into rivers can cause eutrophication. The benefits include price, choice and convenience. Some people also prefer the unblemished appearance and uniformity of intensively farmed foods.

Revision Summary for Module P3 (page 99)

8) After one half-life the count rate will be 420. After another, it will be 210. After another, it will be 105. This takes 4 hours. i.e. 3 half lives = 4 hours

So 1 half-life = 4 ÷ 3 = $1\frac{1}{3}$ hours = 1 hr 20 minutes.

19a) 1000 − (550 + 40 + 28) = 372 J

b) 550 + 50 + 28 = 628 J

c) 372 ÷ 1000 = 0.372

Answers to Extract Questions (page 101)

a) The insulin will remove glucose from their blood — if no food is eaten the blood sugar level may drop too low.

b) The sentence "We believe that our research will improve the lives of the many diabetics who suffer daily and further our scientific understanding." should be ringed.

Index

A

abortion 14
absorbed 59
absorption, of energy 59
accurate result 51
acid rain 20, 22, 23
activity 91
adrenaline 74
adult stem cells 15
aflatoxin 84
air pollution 20, 24
ALARA principle 4, 95
alleles 6-8
alpha particles 90
alpha radiation 89, 91
amino acids 81, 82
amniocentesis 13
animal poo 78
animal research 16
anomalies 47
antibiotics 43
antibodies 40, 41
antigens 40, 41
antioxidants 85
applying scientific knowledge 101
arteries 45
artificial chemicals 80
artificial fertilisers 79
artificial hormones 80
artificial selection 69
artificial sweeteners 85
asexual reproduction 11
asteroid belt 31
asteroids 31, 32
asthma 20
asthma attacks 24
Atlantic 29
atmosphere 18, 20, 32, 34, 62, 63
atmospheric carbon dioxide 102
atoms 19, 60, 89

B

background radiation 93
bacteria 11, 39, 43
belching 1
bequerels (Bq) 91
beta radiation 89, 91
bias 2
Big Bang 36, 37
big craters 32
big molecules 82

biodiversity 76
bitumen 53
black hole 35
blind human trials 44
blood 45, 82
blood group 10
blood sugar 74
blood sugar levels 74, 83
blood vessels 45
bone marrow transplants 15
brain 73
breast cancer 14

C

cancer 10, 61, 92, 93
carbohydrates 81
carbon cycle 64
carbon dioxide 18, 21, 96, 102
carbon dioxide emissions 98
carbon emissions 64
carbon monoxide 21
carrier 12
cars' emissions 25
cassava 84
catalytic converters 25
causal link 24
Central Nervous System (CNS) 73
CGP Exam Simulator 101
chain reaction 97
characteristics 6, 10, 68
chemical reaction 19
chromosomes 6, 7, 9
  sex 9
climate change 32, 102
climate model 65
clinical trials 44
cloning 11
coal 18, 25
cold fusion 2
collision course 29, 32
combustion 19
comets 31
compressive strength 50
computer 26
consensus 5
consequences 4
constant internal environment 74
contamination 92
continental crust 28, 30
controls 86
convection currents 28, 30
core 28, 30

coronary arteries 45
correlation 3, 4, 24, 46, 47, 66
counts per minute (cpm) 91
cracking 53
craters 32
crazy 3
crop rotation 79
crude oil 18, 53
crust 28, 30
crystalline 55
cystic fibrosis 12-14

D

dark matter 36
data-related questions 102
decay 89, 91
decompose 78
defective alleles 12
deforestation 64
density 50
density of gold 51
deoxygenated blood 45
detectors 59
diabetes 15, 83
  type 1 83
  type 2 83
diarrhoea 39
differentiation 15
digestion 6, 82
dinosaurs 32, 75
diseases 10
DNA 6, 41, 68
dodo 76
dominant allele 8, 12
double-blind human trials 44
Down's syndrome 13
drug trials 44

E

Earth 28, 31
earthquake 30
Earth's atmosphere 34
Earth's magnetic field 29
economic factors 5
ecosystem 76
effectors 73
efficiency 95
egg cells 7, 11
elastic 45
electricity 95, 96, 98

Index

electromagnetic (EM) radiation
    34, 58-61, 63, 90
electromagnetic spectrum 58
electrons 89
elongated ellipses 31
embryo 13, 15
emulsifiers 85
enucleated cell 11
environment 10
environmental factors 5
enzymes 6
epidemics 42
epidemiology 46
erosion 28
ethical dilemmas 16
ethics 5
evidence 1-3
evolution 68, 69
expanding universe 36
experiments 1, 24
explanations 29
extinct 68, 75, 76
extract questions 101
eye colour 10

_F_

family tree 12, 72
faulty allele 12
faulty cells 15
first 68
flavour enhancers 85
flavourings 85
flu 43
food additives 85
food colouring 85
Food Standards Agency (FSA) 86
food web 75
fossil fuels 21, 23, 25, 53, 64, 65, 96
fossil records 68, 75
fungi 39, 43
fusion 35

_G_

galaxies 33
gamma radiation 89, 91
gamma rays 90, 93
gene therapy 14
generator 95, 97
genes 6-8, 10
genetic conditions 13
genetic diagram 8, 9

genetic disorder 12-14, 16
genetic manipulation 16
genetic screening 13
genetic tests 13
genetically identical 11
glands 73
global temperature 65, 66
global warming 64, 65
globin 82
glucose 82
gluten 84
glycogen 83
GM crops 86
God 68
Grand Canyon 28
gravity 33, 35
green manure 79
greenhouse effect 20, 63, 96
greenhouse gases 63, 65
growth
    humans 10

_H_

haem 82
haemoglobin 39, 82
hair colour 10
half-life 91, 93
hamsters 8
hardness of a material 50
harvesting crops 79
health 10
health problems 24
healthy diet 87
heart 45
heart attack 45
heart disease 10, 15, 46
herbicides 84, 86
heterocyclic amines (HAs) 84
heterozygous 8
high density polyethene 54
high pressure 45
homeostasis 74
Homo sapiens 72
homozygous 8
hormonal communication 74
hormones 74
Hubble Space Telescope 34
human cells 44
human error 51
Huntington's disorder 12, 13
hurricanes 65
hydrocarbons 18, 19, 53

hypochondriac tendencies 39
hypothesis 1-3

_I_

identical twins 11
immune system 40-42
immunisation 41
impurities 22
infection 40
infertile couples 16
inflammation 39
inflammatory response 40
infrared radiation 58-60, 63
inherited diseases 12
inherited disorders 10
inner core 28
inner planets 31
insulin 83
intelligence 10
intensity of radiation 59
intensive farming 79, 80
interdependence 75
interpreting data 102
ionisation 60
ionising radiation 61, 63, 92
iron 28, 29
irradiation 92
IVF (in vitro fertilisation) 13

_J_

Jupiter 31

_L_

lead aprons 61
lead shields 61
Life Cycle Assessment (LCA) 56
life cycle of stars 35
light detectors 59
light pollution 34
light years 33
limestone 22
limitations 5
lithosphere 28
long chain molecules 55
low density polyethene 54

Index

M

magma 29
magnetic field 28
malaria 39
mammoths 75
man-made (synthetic) materials 49
mantle 28, 30
Mars 31
mass 36
materials 49
materials from animals 49
materials from plants 49
measles 41
measurements 2
medical tracers 95
medicines 76
melamine resin 54
Mercury 31
meteorites 31
meteorologist 29
microbes 40, 78
microorganism 39-41
microwaves 61
Milky Way 33
millions of years 11
millisieverts (mSv) 92
MMR vaccine 41, 42
molecule 21
monomers 54
moons 31
mostly empty space 89
motor neurones 73
mountains 29
mumps 41
muscles 73
mutations 41, 43, 61, 68, 70

N

National Grid 95
natural polymers 81
natural selection 43, 69-71
near-Earth objects (NEOs) 29
negative correlation 47
Neptune 31
nerves 74
nervous communication 74
nervous system 73
neurones 73
neutron star 35
neutrons 89, 90
new 37

nickel 28
nitrogen cycle 78
nitrogen pollution 23
noise pollution 98
North Star 34
nuclear energy 98
nuclear fission 97
nuclear power station 94, 96
nuclear radiation 89, 92
nucleus 6, 11, 89, 91

O

observations 1, 29, 37
oceanic crust 28, 30
offspring 8
orbits 31
organic farming 79, 80
organic waste 78
outer core 28
outer planets 31
outer space 68
outliers 51
oxygenated blood 45
ozone layer 63

P

Paper Four, Ideas In Context 103
parasites 39
particulate carbon 21
pathogens 39
penetrate 90
perfectly safe 93
pesticides 84, 86
pests and diseases 80
petrol 53
photons 58, 60
photosynthesis 62, 64
placebo 44
planets 31, 33
plasticisers 55
Pluto 31
point of view 2
poisonous chemicals 84
pollen levels 24
pollutants 20, 21
pollution 34
polycyclicaromatic hydrocarbons (PAHs) 84
polymerise 54
polymers 54, 55, 81
polypropylene 54

polystyrene foam 54
power stations 95, 98
pre-implantation genetic diagnosis 13
precautionary principle 4
precautions 95
preservatives 85
probability 9
products 20
product's properties 52
properties 20
proteins 81, 82
protons 89
protostar 31, 35
protozoa 39
PVC 54

R

rabbits 69
radiation 34, 58, 89, 91, 95
  penetrating power 90
radiation sickness 61
radio waves 62
radioactive 89, 91, 97
radioactive decay 28, 30
random 89
reactants 20
reading graphs 102
reading the right scale 102
real world 100
receptors 73
recessive 8
recessive allele 12
recommended daily amounts 87
recycling 78
red giant 35
reducing pollution 25
refinery gas 53
reflected 59
reflection 59
regular moderate exercise 46
reliable 2
renewable energy resources 97
renewable fuel sources 98
renewable resources 26
reproducible 1, 2
reproductive cells 16
resources 75
respiration 64
risk 4, 94
rock cycle 30
rubber 49
rubella 41

Index

S

safer 25
Sankey diagrams 95
satellites 29, 32
Saturn 31
science based technology 26
scientific community 37
scientific controversy 71
scientific insight 101
scientific research 26
scientific study 3
scientists 1
sedimentary rocks 28
selective breeding 69
sense organs 73
sensory neurones 73
sex cells 7
sexual reproduction 11
sickle cell anaemia 15
sieverts (Sv) 92
skin cancer 61, 66
small intestine 82
smaller molecules 82
smallpox 42
social factors 5
Soil Association 80
solar power 96
Solar System 28, 31, 33
space 33
specialised 15
species on Earth 68
speed of light 59
sperm 7
spinal cord 73
spinal injuries 15
splitting atoms 96
sporting ability 10
stabilisers 85
stable isotopes 89
staphylococcus 39
starch 82
stars 31, 33, 35
statistical correlation 24
steam 95, 97
stem cell research 15
stem cells 15
sterilise 93
stiff material 50
stimulus 73
stonefly larvae 75
structural proteins 6

sufferer 12
suitability of different materials 52
sulfur 22, 25
Sun 31, 33, 35
sunbathing 66
sunlight 62
sunscreen/sunblock 66
supercontinent 29
supernova 35
survival of the fittest 69
sustainable development 26
symbol equations 19
symmetrical pattern 29
symptoms 39
synthetic leather 54

T

target cells 74
tectonic plates 30
telescopes 29, 32
temperature control 74
tension (or tensile) strength 50
testing 2
theory 1
thermal insulators 54
tick the box questions 100
totally indisputable fact 2
toxic 20
toxins 39
trajectory 32
transmission 59
trial by evidence 2
tricky questions 100
turbine 95, 97

U

unanswerable questions 5
underlining 101
unique melting point 50
universe 33, 36
unstable 91
unstable isotopes 89
unstable nuclei 91
Uranus 31
urine 82
UV radiation 66

V

vaccination 42
vacuum 59
valid research 3
valves 45
variation 10, 69
veins 45
Venus 31
viruses 14, 39, 43
visual pollution 98
volcanoes 30

W

waste
   nuclear 97
water levels 74
white dwarf 35
wildlife habitats 98
wind turbines 26, 96
works properly 74
world's population 26

X

X chromosome 9
X-ray 60

Y

Y chromosome 9